The Self-Love Project

How to finally fall in love with yourself

Gabrielle G.

Cover by Gabrielle G.
Poems and Formatting by Gabrielle G.

First Printing, 2022
ISBN: 978-1-7774882-5-3
Ebook: 978-1-7774882-6-0

Gabrielle G.
PO 40527
Kirkland, QC
H9H 5G8 CANADA
www.authorgabrielleg.com

Contents

Introduction

The Self-Love Project: How To Finally Fall In Love With Yourself
   By Gabrielle G.

"Once upon a time, I did everything for others to love me while not loving myself unconditionally. The result was heartbreakingly painful. But I don't regret anything; I've learned, I've grown, and now I love myself." – Gabrielle G.

Through her personal story, poetry, meditation and journaling exercises, Gabrielle G. brings you on a journey of self-love, so you never feel rejected, abandoned, unlovable, or unworthy ever again. In ten chapters, you will discover who you are, change the narrative of your story, fall in love with yourself and be who you always wanted to be. So, grab a pen and a journal, sit comfortably, and take a leap of faith. This book is only the beginning of your most beautiful love story.

When you love yourself
Everything falls around you
Exactly where it's meant to be
And you don't need to push
Rose thorns down others' throats
To finally feel loved and worthy
Of the petals you carry.

Gabrielle G.

Foreword

Before you start this self-love journey with me, let me tell you who I am. Once upon a time, I did everything for others to love me while not loving myself unconditionally. The result was heartbreakingly painful. But I don't regret anything; I've learned, I've grown, and now I love who I am.

The truth is, I am no one and I am everyone.

I am not a psychotherapist, a psychologist, or a doctor. I am not a self-help leader who has been giving conferences about loving yourself for years. I am a woman who didn't love herself for about forty years, who found a way to do so through therapy, and also through rewriting the narrative of her own life.

I am a mother, a poet, an author, a survivor, a friend, and a lover, and I want to share my journey to help others in their healing recovery. I am no one and everyone, and in finding love, I found peace. I found a way to love myself and to stop my demons ruling my life.

Here is my first advice: take this book with a grain of salt. Take what resonates and leave what doesn't, or come back to it later.

Loving yourself is not an easy path to choose, but such a rewarding one to walk down.

Whatever you need healing from, know that the answer is mostly in loving yourself more. I want to help you see your own worth.

Nonetheless, let me tell you something important before we start. If you are suffering, if you are depressed or in an extremely dark place, if you need support, I urge you to talk to someone in the medical field.

I have tried many, many, many alternative ways of healing on my journey, but nothing has replaced psychotherapy.

Now, let's begin our journey.

Through poetry, meditation, journaling, and sharing my own story, I will try to guide you in discovering your awesomeness. There is no right or wrong way to do this; there is only pride in meeting ourselves for the first time and finally falling in love with who we truly are.

So, take a pen and a journal, sit down comfortably, calm your mind, and take a step towards what might be the best love story of your life.

XO,
   Gabrielle

"Very little grows on jagged rock. Be ground, be crumbled, so wildflowers will come up where you are."

—Rumi

Chapter 1

Unbuilding Your House of Lies

H*i, my name is Gabrielle, and I am an addict.*

THIS IS NOT HOW I THOUGHT I WOULD INTRODUCE myself. I generally start by saying that I am an author, a poet, a mother and that I truly believe me telling my journey can help you walk yours.

Being an addict is not what defines me, but through the months I worked on loving myself I accepted that it is part of who I am.

I already knew I have an addictive personality, and I never drank to profusion and never used drugs to the point of losing touch with reality because I saw the damages of this kind of addiction on friends and family. And, to be honest, because I was always too scared to lose control. Despite this, I recognize that I am an addict and I work daily on keeping balance and peace centered in my life.

What was I addicted to? The most addictive drug humans will ever try to get sober from: Love.

And, to be honest, I still am.

For as long as I can remember, I looked for the high of being loved in every relationship I entered. I looked for unconditional love, with no other care in the world. I searched under the piles of frogs I kissed, wanting to become their princess. I jumped from friend-ship to friendship, held on to people I shouldn't be holding on to, begged, sobbed, and pushed so I could feel the rush of the dose. The highs were magical, but the lows? Oh, the lows were hard and always made me ques-tion my worth. If someone didn't love me, I took it to mean that I was not worth of love. I thought I was the one at fault. I found everything I did wrong and continued blaming myself until I had shattered my own heart.

As you can imagine, this was a major problem.

I truly thought that for me to be worthy of living, I needed to be loved by others.

I fully believed that if others loved me, I wouldn't feel like a failure.

I utterly assumed that another loving me was my only salvation.

Over the years, I hid this deep insecurity under sarcasm, humor, confidence, and a certain coldness that I explained as "being guarded." I was the first one to say that I didn't easily open to people when, in fact, I was dying for them to dig into my story, to show me love and attention.

I accepted bad love and put myself in disrespectful situations because I thought that was all I was worthy of.

I built a wall around myself, complete with fiery hoops at the top that climbers had to jump through. I made it so hard to break in to see the real me that I wouldn't feel disappointed if no one succeeded or even tried. But then, I kept giving the climbers water to quench the fire, so that I wouldn't end up alone.

As you can imagine, I was a mess.

"You accept the love you think you deserve," my best friend said one day, quoting *The Perks of Being a Wallflower*.

How right she was.

I accepted breadcrumbs, and silences, and coldness, and betrayal, while continuously giving more because I was so afraid to be unlovable.

I never held boundaries for fear of not being loved and gave thousands of chances for people to step harder on my heart, abandoning myself every time I did so.

I pretended not to care about most things while silently crying at night about them.

I embraced a life I thought I wanted because I was told that I was hard to love, that I should be happy to have found someone who wanted to marry me, someone who loved me so much.

I created who I was from the idea people had of me. I learned at a young age that I wasn't worthy of being loved because I was, and I quote, "so difficult," and I was always "taking up so much space." For years, I thought that I was everything that was wrong in my family.

It took me forty years and a good amount of therapy and self-reflection to arrive where I am today. It took me three years of hell and liters of tears to discard the preconceived notions I had of myself. It took me wanting to die to learn how to love myself.

The truth is, I wasn't difficult. I bent myself backwards to be accepted. I almost never said what I truly thought, and when I did, I apologized profusely because of my fear of being rejected, abandoned, excluded.

I was a people pleaser, always trying to fit in. I was a chameleon, changing my colors to match those around me, trying to find love and acceptance. I was a full of lies, wearing a mask of indifference even though I was hurting physically daily, eaten by anxiety to my core, trying to find a way to be loved, to finally feel I had found my tribe.

I was a bomb ready to explode and a heart about to stop.

And as far as I can remember, that's how I felt my whole life.

I don't think anyone really knew me, except maybe one or two people. Even then, I was never who I was meant to be, but rather the person I had created to survive.

Nonetheless, I had a happy life. I got married and felt loved and chosen for a hot minute. The high was luke-warm as I never got a proposal; but still, I was proving my worth as someone was marrying me before I was thirty, which my family insisted was a blessing, considering who I was. And then I had three beautiful children who gave me the high of unconditional love.

In a way, the magic of motherhood delayed years of healing.

PEOPLE WILL TELL YOU I HAVE A FUSIONAL relationship with my children, especially my oldest. I don't think so, but again, I let people think whatever they want and I don't fight their opinion of me, not anymore. What people don't know is how by becoming a mother, I found what I considered a perfect love through the eyes of a human being. I was so desperate to be loved that becoming a mother gave me the best high of my life.

Better than my marriage, which I went into thinking I could always divorce. Better than being a daughter myself, as I had learned love was very conditional in my family, and I always felt like a bother, a mistake, a burden to my parents. Better than those friendships I always got entangled in that had always finished in heartbreaks since forever because I was too loyal, too clingy, too direct.

Those babies...they saved me.

My husband was travelling a lot at the time and wasn't around much (though when present, he was and still is an incredible father) so it was easy to become my kids' everything.

I could love and be loved forever, if I didn't mess it up. And because I was adamant to prove to anyone that I was better than my family, I promised myself that I wouldn't mess it up.

Fast-forward a handful of years later to an international move, to having to recreate my circle of people, to realizing I had become everything I didn't want to be, and children were becoming more independent, and I was craving love again.

Those loving babies were now almost teenagers and their unconditional love was more conditional than the love of my cat. Don't get me wrong, I have wonderful children. But as the hugs became sparse, their need for mommy changed and my name became mom, and the days and their stacks of problems were never ending, my addiction wasn't fulfilled anymore.

And so, despite my loving husband and three adorable children, I started to spiral.

I had a job that didn't satisfy me, but I kept it longer than I should have because I was good at it.

When I finally changed career and started to write romance novels, I felt out of place all the time, like an imposter who couldn't succeed because I didn't write what was expected. That feeling consumed my mind.

I literally asked friends to love me, though I didn't think I was worthy of their love.

I gave, and gave, and gave, and the more I gave, the more I spiraled down, like a frantic addict trying to find her fix and not getting it. The more I spiraled, the less I felt love, and the more I looked for it in all the wrong places with people who couldn't love me fully, with some who lied, used, and manipulated me, and others who weren't emotionally available.

Of course, I hid it all under smiles and humor, but deep down I needed constant reassurance; it was exhausting for me and for my entourage.

And it didn't get better. In fact, it got worse.

Depression, suicidal thoughts, anxiety... My demons had eaten me alive.

But with everything crumbling down around me, I was finally able to see myself for who I was: an addict.

AN ADDICT WHO DIDN'T LOVE HERSELF.

An addict who was wearing a mask at all time.

An addict I wasn't proud of.

An addict I didn't even like.

An addict I would have never hang out with.

I WROTE THIS POEM BACK THEN, WHEN THE MASK started to crack, and my demons took over in place of my survival mode, which I had been in for forty years.

It took many months after this for me to really step into who I was and to be proud of myself, but this was the start of it all, of recognizing that I wasn't who I wanted to be, of knowing that I didn't like who I had become and that I wasn't aligned with anything I wanted to be.

It was a hard truth to write, and I hope this resonates with you a little.

Gabrielle G.

The Mask

* * *

Behind my mask is a cemetery
Of all the scars inflicted to my heart
They still ooze the hurt necessary
For every love story to fall apart

Behind my smile is a dungeon
Where I keep my happiness captive
It tastes a lot like corruption
But makes me feel attractive

Behind my eyes is a longing
That you will never understand
'Cause your words are sharpening
my hopes to die at your hands

Behind my mask is another me
That I thought you could love
Behind my tears is someone no one sees
Someone, I'm not proud of.

Excerpt from To The Man I Loved too
Much, *by Gabrielle G.*

CAN YOU BELIEVE THAT THE PERSON WRITING A BOOK about how to fall in love with yourself is the same person who wrote that poem?

Thinking of who I was when I wrote these lines shatters my heart.

I was so broken.

I felt so unworthy of love, of happiness.

I thought I couldn't be loved for who I was.

I thought that everything that was happening to me was deserved and that all I deserved was to die.

And so, for every failed relationship, I took all the blame I could. I carried all the weight. I fell into a deep, self-loathing depression, and I pushed people away until some indeed stopped loving me.

I was needy.

I was unhappy.

I was broken.

I couldn't get back up, but I was too proud to ask for help...

It was a pattern I had gone through before, in my twenties, over and over, and now in my forties, I was back at it. Or, had I never stopped feeling that way?

Here is a truth: when we don't love ourselves, we tend to push away people who love us, simply because we can't understand why they love us.

And so, one of the most crucial steps in journey of self-love—and one of the hardest steps, too—is to understand why people love us.

To do so, you must unbuild the house of lies you created to survive.

Do you know what I mean? This house you've built to justify your actions so that you can hide those feelings of unworthiness and self-loathing that are eating at your soul. The blame you've put on others, not understanding that they were only mirroring your own traumas. The things you did to justify the fact that those people pushed you away or didn't chose you, or hurt you. Those lies that surround your true self, the ones that form walls between yourself and others, the ones that make you "strong," "untouchable," or "right." The ugly lies we tell ourselves so we can justify anything, just as long as we don't have to feel.

For a few months, nothing changed.

I was dying of a slow, silent depression and I continued sinking into the unhealthiest ways of living. I stayed silent. I didn't share how I felt. I thought no one cared…not even the love of my life.

My self-depreciation was high.

My abandonment issues were ringing the doorbell of my house of lies daily.

I felt alone, forsaken, and I created stories in my head, telling myself that all of this was proof that no one loved me. And, as my phone was dead silent after buzzing constantly for years, I took it as another proof that no one cared, that my life wasn't worth anything.

It went on and on and on.

One night, while crying myself to sleep, I asked myself a question between sobs. That question let light enter the darkness of my mind:

Why was I so afraid to be loved?

Something clicked. It opened the door to other questions.

What was the fear that held me at gunpoint? Why did I fear people knowing who I really was?

I wasn't a serial killer, hiding bodies in my basement.

I wasn't a horrible person, strangling pets as a hobby.

I wasn't someone who thrived in hurting others.

I was a lost soul, a child who thought she had never been loved, an addict who needed to find her next fix, an emotional vampire feeding on my own feeling of unworthiness, but I wasn't not worth knowing, not worth loving, not worth ghosting.

And so, I dug into that uncontrollable fear of being abandoned, and every time I found a new fear behind the rock of my survival, I asked myself why, and then I challenged my answer and asked "why" again.

I didn't sleep that night. I went deeper, and deeper, and deeper, until I found the roots of my problem. It was a dark room in my house of lies, but the moment I opened the door, I poured light on my darkest secrets and felt instantly better. The light I was shining—the light of acknowledgement that I needed for my life to change, — became a beacon for the rest of the journey.

This is an important step, and I invite you to journal about it...but maybe don't wait until you are crying your eyes out in the middle of a sleepless night to do so.

THERE ARE EASIER WAYS TO WORK ON YOURSELF. Here is one.

Ask yourself:

What am I afraid of, and why?

What is it that makes me not love myself?

What is it that makes me not treat myself the way I treat others (if you treat others with respect), or why am I as cruel to others as I am to myself?

It's only in destroying the house of lies we built to protect ourselves that we can find the foundation of loving who we truly are.

I'm not blaming you for creating lies about who you are. I did it for years.

I wasn't a pathological liar, but I lied every time I said yes to things I didn't want to do. I was a liar every time I made fun of someone that had the same hidden insecurities I had. I was a liar every time I gossiped or said I was fine when I wasn't.

We all want to find some control.

We are all afraid to be judged, to be laughed at, not to conform, and not to be loved; this is normal for most of us.

But it's only in seeing who our true self is that we can fall in love with who we truly are.

It's only by hearing our most troubling, darkest thoughts and facing our most terrifying fears that we can fight our demons and shine light on them, so that love can enter us through the same wounds we have been bleeding from for years. As Rumi says, *"The wound is the place where the light enters you."*

It's only by embracing our truth that we can fight our lies.

I invite you to read the following instructions first, and then do the exercise. (Most exercises and meditations in this book will be set up this way.) You can also record yourself reading the instructions and then press play when you have a minute to work on yourself. Whatever you prefer.

Exercise 1: Introduce yourself

Sit comfortably on a chair with your feet on the ground, or on the floor in a crossed-legged position.

Take a big breath in through your nose, hold it while you count to three, and then let it go from your mouth. Repeat this a couple of times until you feel the burden of pretense lifting from your shoulders.

Remember you are safe here, there is no judgement.

Continue breathing slowly, and then imagine you are facing yourself, as if you were meeting someone for the first time.

Look into your own eyes and say, "Hi, my name is XXX, and I am..." and let the word come out naturally. Don't think about making it right, don't overthink it, just let out whatever you need to say about yourself that you aren't proud of.

The first time I did this exercise, it came out as, "Hi, my name is Gabrielle and I am a fake." Harsh words to say about myself... Was I fake? I don't think so, but that's how I felt about myself.

This is where the "other you" comes in. Let's call it the *positive side of you*.

This You steps in to answer the question with something you're proud of.

"No, I am XXX, and I am..." This should be a positive statement, pride should lift your spirit, light should push away the darkness of the first statement. This should be something good that you can't deny about yourself.

Mine was "No, I am Gabrielle, and I am kind-hearted." But it could be that you're a good cook, you're a good friend, you are pretty, you are smart, you are talented at whatever it is that you love to do. Find something good about yourself.

Then sit in silence, and hear yourself think. In our day and age, we often do everything we can not to hear ourselves think anymore.

So, here, I want you to sit with no music, no TV, no social media, no kids, no nothing, just you and your thoughts so you can analyze if they are positive or negative. If they are dragging you down or lifting you up. If you are forming a smile on your lips or a frown between your eyes.

If they are negative thoughts, remember the positive word that *the positive side of you* used. Project that word outward, imagine it being inked on your skin, dancing around you, shouted by strangers on the street as you walk by. "Here is XXXX, and she makes a sick, yummy brownie!"

Think of a specific moment when you thought this positive thought about yourself. Go back to this moment, imagine taking a bite of that brownie, and be proud of it.

Stay in the feeling of pride. Feel your heart getting bigger with positive thoughts about yourself.

If the thoughts that come up naturally are positive, embrace those thoughts, dance with them, play with them, and smile. Allow yourself to feel good.

Stay there a little more. Enjoy the moment.

Take another big breath, come back slowly to yourself, open your eyes, and acknowledge that this pride you felt, is the first step of self-love.

Then, take a pen and paper and make a list of those good things you thought about yourself. Make a list of things you are good at. These thoughts and this list will be a tool every time you feel bad about yourself, a sort of happy place to go to in order to lift your spirit and vibrations.

You can do the journaling and the meditation as many times as you need. It will help you destroy the house of lies you have built and live in, and it will help you to slowly shape a new house of love.

Don't be afraid to go deeper, it only opens yourself to love. And this is the goal after all, no?

Now, close this book and go do something you love to reward yourself for the light you let in.

Next chapter, we'll fight those lies a little more, showing you the Monster that lives inside of you and how to fight it with its own reflection.

* * *

Scorch the earth of your fears
and build a kingdom on their ashes
and when the wind burns your eyes
remember my whispers:
only you can muffle your doubts
only you can fight your demons
only you know your true worth.
So, adjust your crown
and sit on your throne
and with love on your lips
smile...

Gabrielle G.

Chapter 2

Rebuilding Yourself One Truth at a Time

After working on unbuilding the house of lies we've created around ourselves, it is now time to build the foundation of loving ourselves with stones of truth.

When we look at ourselves in a mirror, we tend to believe our own lies.

Lies of unworthiness for some of us, or lies about feeling fine when we deeply aren't.

I truly believe that if you are reading this book, it's because you want to heal, you want to love yourself, you want to find a way to mend your soul, so I won't try to convince you that you need to work on yourself if you believe you don't.

If this is your state of mind, close the book and continue with your life. I wasn't ready for years, and you can't push anyone to do the work.

But if you still believe you aren't worthy of happiness, and joy, and love, and anything that can make you feel good, it is time to take the little truth *the positive side of you* whispered in last chapter's meditation and build a new you that you will fall in love with.

FOR THIS CHAPTER, ALL YOU WILL NEED IS A MIRROR — preferably clean, so maybe some Windex as well—and yourself.

When I started to want to feel better, to find a solution to the heartache and soul-break I was in, I realized I needed to have a deep look at myself.

So, one day, I stood in front of my bathroom mirror and looked deeply into my dejected blue eyes.

Everyone who knew me in my twenties would tell you that I avoided eye contact at all times. I had grown out of this habit when I discovered that I could get my dose of love by looking into the eyes of the ones I loved. Sometimes it was just a glimmer, but I could sit and look deep into the eyes of someone who I knew loved me...

Looking into my own eyes, though, was different. I could always see all the ugliness I was trying to hide.

So, I stood there, looking at myself. Looking at those wrinkles that seemed so much more pronounced than a few months before. Looking at that nose, which I was never crazy about. Looking at my scars that I never did anything to hide but hate with a passion. Looking at me, the whole me, this woman of forty-something who was drowning and didn't have the strength to save herself anymore.

Again, I was ready to try anything to feel that I was

deserving of love, and if you are as low as I was, know that I am already proud of you for the steps to come.

Because I was ready to try anything, I looked at myself and said, "I love you."

My eyes started to water, my throat clogged, my brain fogged. I couldn't bear it, and I jumped into the shower and cried under the stream of hot water for a good fifteen minutes.

I let it all out. It was one of my ugliest cries ever.

I had never told myself I loved me. Never. Ever.

After the shower, I didn't want to look at myself in the mirror.

Nonetheless, I am a woman who loves her eyeliner and I kind of had to look at my reflection to draw a line on my eyelids.

First, I avoided my own image. But once both eyes were lined with charcoal grey and the mascara was applied, I looked at myself for a final glance to be sure it wasn't a disaster. My eyes carried a despondency that still haunts me when I think about it, but my make-up was on point. I closed my eyes, took a deep breath, and released it in a sigh that everyone could have heard from Montreal to Paris, and when I opened my eyes, I said it again.

"I Love you, Gab."

This time, my heart sank a little, my stomach twirled, but the corners of my lips turned up.

I tried again.

"You are a beautiful lost soul, and I love you."

I nodded to myself and my heart felt a little lighter.

I didn't insist anymore; I didn't want to ruin the

makeup by crying because I pushed myself too much. As important as it is to push yourself, it is even more important to know when to stop.

I didn't talk to myself in the mirror again for at least a week. It was one of those things that you know is good for you and you feel good doing it, but the commitment...? I wasn't ready for it, and I caught myself a few times, being unable to look into my own eyes. I wasn't ready to love myself. I felt the emotion overwhelming.

At the time, I wasn't meditating daily like I am now. I was still afraid to sit with myself.

I was thinking, writing, frantically trying to understand why I was so alone, and feeling like everything was my fault, and again asking how and why, and why and how...

Of course, I overthought the experience and focused on the negative of it.

Truth is, I wasn't ready to discover the amazing truth about myself.

I wasn't ready to shine.

If you find yourself in the same position, that's okay; this chapter might take time, energy, and tears. I've been there. I've believed the lies I told myself. I believed the worst because I was afraid of what people would think, would do, would say...

Those were all lies I told myself because I didn't feel worthy of love.

But I was; I am.

AND YOU ARE, TOO.

Believe me, you are. Everyone is.

I wrote a poem about this feeling of unworthiness when I truly believed I was nothing of what is written in it. I called it "Lies in the Mirror" because I didn't think any of those lines were true. But now I believe every line, and on days when I feel a little low, I recite it with pride, and I feel love and light hug me instantly.

Lies in the Mirror

* * *

I love you.
You are enough.
You are bright.
You are brilliant.
You are beautiful.
You deserve love.
I love you.
You are enough.
You are bright.
You are brilliant.
You are beautiful.
You are...

Excerpt from Melancholy & Cinnamon,
by Gabrielle G.

THE THING IS, IT IS ALWAYS EASIER TO BELIEVE THE bad thoughts about ourselves than the good ones. I am sure you've realized this already. Someone can tell you ten good things, but you will believe the one negative comment someone else made. I dealt with this a lot with the reviews of my books. I always kept in mind the one bad review instead of the good ones. It's the same with the *positive side of you* versus the *Monster side of you*.

We've met your positive side in chapter one. And you've lived with your Monster for a while, even if you haven't named it yet.

I call it the Monster, but some call it the ego, or the little man in our head, or the saboteur. You know that voice that whispers our unworthiness and feeds off our fears? That little voice that told you in chapter one that you were not good, that disagreed with the positive way you presented yourself? That's the Monster that we are trying to fight here. That little voice we've internalized that prefers to see us fail so we can stay safe in our beliefs of unworthiness. It's an auto-protection device that we can't switch off and that has bullied us into trusting it. It's a smart, sneaky snake who likes to ruin every good thing. It's why we accept other people's unacceptable behavior towards us, and why we can't believe we deserve the good things, and why we feel like shit most of the time.

I call it the Monster because it is an ugly beast whispering the worst things about ourselves. I call it the Monster because it casts a shadow on every good moment, and if we manage to enjoy ourselves, it's what leaves us waiting for the other shoe to drop. I call it the

Monster, because I always dreamed of slaying dragons with a sword of love.

Take a moment to think about your Monster.

What does yours say?

What does yours try to ruin?

Here is what my Monster told me over and over for months:

About losing friends and love: *I deserve it because I'm hard to love.*

About not reaching my sales goals: *This is normal for me because I'm a failure.*

When my kids getting in trouble: *What was I expecting? I am a bad mother.*

The Monster's thoughts are dark and twisty, and rooted to the deepest of our traumas. They are there to hold us back. Its words are masked as our truth, but they are lies that we have been conditioned to believe.

That's why we introduced ourselves as fake or whatever negative word you used to introduce yourself as in chapter one, because our Monster is dominant.

That's why it may have been so hard to accept those good things you had to say about yourself, because our Monster likes to take charge of our narrative.

Speaking of those good things that the *positive side of you* said about you in chapter one, I asked you to write them down, and I truly hope you did.

Because now it's time for your next exercise.

Exercise 2: Mirror Talk

Face your mirror and say the first positive thing you said about yourself in chapter one. See how you feel about it. Reflect on it. Repeat it a couple of times while looking into your own eyes. If this is too much, stop here. Take a big breath and walk away. If you think you can take more love, continue going through the list, saying the positive words aloud to yourself. Once you've gone through the whole list, say, "I love you." And check how you feel now.

Let me remind you that, except for the "I love you" that I asked you to say, those words are yours. You believed them before and you should still believe them now. Those are the foundation of your house of truth. Those words came from you.

The "I love you" may still be a little tricky, but because it is preceded by words that you believe, you can take this first step toward accepting it as a truth.

Come back to this exercise as many times as you need. Positive affirmations help us trick the Monster and shine love into its eyes. This is the only way to fight the Monster, the only way to make it smaller, the only way to stop believing its lies.

To finish this important chapter, I would like to invite you to meditate. Again, if this last exercise overwhelmed you, just take a big breath and close the book. You can come back to it another time.

But, if you feel that you have a little more energy to give yourself some love, don't hesitate to sit quietly and to take a big breath. Hold for the count of three and exhale again. Visualize yourself the way you see yourself at your best. Smile at yourself. Continue breathing. Smile a little more.

Now, calm your thoughts and slowly whisper these words:

I love you.

You are enough.

You are bright.

You are brilliant.

You are beautiful.

You deserve love.

And that's why I love you.

Take another big breath and let the feeling of unworthiness leave your soul.

Eyes still closed, repeat these words a few more times.

I love you.

You are enough.

You are bright.

You are brilliant.

You are beautiful.
You deserve love.
And that's why I love you.

Breathe in and out slowly.
Let love fill you.
Let the light in.
Don't be shy.
Don't be scared to cry.
Don't judge yourself.
Let it all flow.
Let it all go.

And, sit with every emotion. Take your time, feel each sentence, visualize all of them hugging you, holding you, and allowing the love you feel, even if it's a tiny, tiny seed, to make you smile.

Don't fake smile to please me; I have no ball in your game. Smile because you are loved, because you are enough, bright, brilliant, and beautiful.

Plant this little seed inside your heart. With some attention, it will bloom and to transform you from inside. Water it with this meditation, make it grow and allow love to make you feel worthy.

Take one last big breath. Release it all. Open your eyes and feel the peace and light surrounding you.

Congratulations, you just gave yourself some love.

And, to show you that letting some light in works, read the poem below.

I wrote it once things became clearer.

Remember that where there is light, there
is love.
So always keep some light shining on your
Monster. Let it whisper all it wants,
but don't believe what it has to say.
(I'll teach you how in the next
chapter.)
Tell yourself the positive things about
yourself as often as you can.
And when the Monster's screams are too
loud, adopt this mantra:
Where there is light, there is love.
Where there is light, there is love.
Where there is light, there is love....

And start talking to yourself like you talk to your friends when they are feeling down because, rumor has it, you are your own best friend. It's time you start treating yourself this way.

Whispered Truce

* * *

Counting your blessings
On the tips of your fingers
Murmur your depression
Like a dirty prayer.

It's easy to forget
How much one is loved
While choking on threats
Under sadness' gloves.

Focus on the light
Let it bathe your wounds
Hold yourself tight
Call back your howling hounds.

Accept your truce
That comes with shivers
Push away your self-abuse
And start smiling in the mirror.
Excerpt from *Melancholy & Cinnamon* by Gabrielle G.

Chapter 3

Keep Your Eyes on the Prize

"Friendship is the purest love" – Osho.

Do you have a best friend, a close friend, a sister, or anyone else who always lifts you up and listens to you when you need them? Someone who is there for you when you feel low, when you feel the world is a little heavier to carry, and the only way out is to speak your truth?

It took me a long time to find her, but I do. This friend always listens to me and never judges me. She is compassionate and understanding, and even if she sometimes gets into her own head, she still finds time to choose me over and over again.

But, this wasn't always the case.

She wasn't always like that with me. At some point in my life, she told me that I was fake, and fat, and ugly, and full of wrinkles, and stupid, and an imposter, and that I deserved to die, and that it was to be expected that no one loved me because I was such an asshole to the world. She said that I really deserved everyone walking away out of my life because I was a piece of shit under the shoe of people I loved.

Tough talk, isn't it?

Well, here is the thing, my actual best friend would NEVER say those things to me. NEVER. And I'm pretty sure most of us would never stay friends with someone who treated us that way.

Now, what if I tell you that I am my actual best friend? What if I tell you that I used to talk to myself that way? What if I insist that those cruel words were deserved because that is how I felt about myself?

Are those deprecating words more acceptable?

Do you find this normal?

Is it something you do, too?

I want you to think about it. If we don't talk to our besties, sisters, or anyone else that way, why would we do so to ourselves?

Why can't we tell ourselves to fuck off?

I'm not saying I never do this anymore, or that you should feel like a failure if you do it, too. Shit happens. This happened to me just this morning as I wrote those lines.

So, who am I to teach you to love yourself when I sometimes still struggle with self-love, even while writing a book about finally falling in love with yourself?

Who am I to tell people it's a process when I still feel bad looking at the wrinkles around my eyes?

Who am I to...? You see what I mean? It's easy to fall back on the old habits and thoughts that don't serve the new us we want to become.

Even if we aren't on a healing journey, we all have intrusive, dark, or crazy thoughts that we don't follow through or don't believe. Our job is to push them away and find a way not to believe our Monster.

Here is an example most people have and don't follow through on, "I'm going to kill my partner!"

We have all said or thought this. Nonetheless, our partners are still breathing, and we haven't even come up with a plan yet, nor a place to hide the body.

Why? Because we didn't listen to that thought. We didn't jump on the idea of sharpening our knives, or believe our own disturbing whisper that tells us to use them. We simply didn't follow through.

We threw our partner and whatever maddening thing they did to the back of what is called our *mental bus* and moved on, with our eyes still on the road and without giving the thought of killing them the time of the day.

To understand the concept of the mental bus, imagine yourself driving a bus full of passengers.

Some are rowdy teenagers, some are kids, some are old little ladies, some are sleeping, others are just reading quietly, etc.

You get the picture.

You are the driver of that bus, focusing on the road in

front of you, your hands perfectly settled on the steering wheel.

Suddenly, one of the rowdy teenagers screams that you're fat and ugly.

It hurts your feelings, of course, and you try to defend yourself, but you babble something inaudible while looking toward the back.

It's not helping, and you swirl a little off the road, but you're still okay.

But because you almost lost control and the passengers saw an opportunity to rattle you more, another teenager follows up, saying that you suck, and right away a third one says you're stupid and not good at anything.

The children make a song out of it that they chant loudly.

"You suck! You're ugly and stupid."

The rest of the bus passengers join.

The teenagers are dancing in the aisle, moving toward you.

You feel overwhelmed.

Everything is a freaking mess.

Your attention is on the teenagers and their behavior, and as you turn to try to stop whatever is happening you lose total control of the bus and it tumbles into a valley of darkness.

Your eyes weren't on the prize. Your eyes left the road. Your mind let the Monster win. Game over. (Insert Game Over music.)

Now, let's rewind.

Imagine the same teenager screaming that you're

ugly, and you having only to raise your hand for him to stop.

Why does he stop?

Because in your hand is a beam of light that burns his mouth and makes him mute. Because this is not a situation you will allow to escalate.

Because you don't want to fall into a valley of darkness.

This is your life, your dream, your self-love story, and you are not available to entertain the negative thoughts screaming for attention in your mind. You are driving the bus of your life, your thoughts are the passengers who ride with you, and you need to get to your destination.

You need to be in the moment.

You need to choose you.

So, you raise your hand and use your light to render that rude, rowdy thought mute.

Stopping bullying yourself is this easy.

You might not think it is, but I am here to tell you it's true.

If you've ever stood up for someone, if you've ever asked anyone to stop what they were doing, you already know how to do this . You do the exact same with yourself.

The first time I used this method, I wasn't sure it would work. It was not long after I went through a friendship breakup, and I had taken every word that this brand-new exfriend told me as a definition of my character.

We often speak about romantic break-ups, but for me, friendship breakups are far more hurtful, especially as adults when we are supposed to have our life together and have found our tribe. I had really thought that friend would be in my life for a very long time.

Anyway, I believed that friend who had walked away and had told me to fuck off while I was in the midst of fighting my depression, self-loathing spiral and anxiety.

What exactly happened between us is still something I don't totally understand. She has her version of the facts and I have mine. The truth is somewhere in between. I don't pretend I know, and neither do I want to anymore.

As you can imagine, my self-love crumbled, and what I was telling myself at the time was destructive. Nonetheless, I continued repeating these things to myself.

I believed that I was the worst friend ever, a failure of a mother, the shittiest woman on the planet, a bad person who treated people like shit. And, because this had happened with someone who I considered like a sister, I distanced myself from my other friends, too, thinking that I was harming every one of them with who I had become. I thought I was the cause of everything bad happening around me, and that I deserved to die alone. My marriage was at its lowest, my neediness—even though I didn't want to burden my entourage with it—was at its highest. It was a complex situation, and I often felt that I couldn't breathe anymore. I would just lie down on the floor and let everything fall apart around me.

Trying to grasp onto anything to help me survive and to feel a little lighter, I started to walk in nature. These walks generally ended with me in tears, losing every battle against myself...but I kept trying. It was sad and ugly, and a very dark period of my life, but the walks did help release what needed to be healed.

On a beautiful, sunny, winter day after a snowfall, I decided to go walk alone in the nature park near where I live.

The air was crisp but the sun warm. The freshly fallen white coat of snow and the shiny blue of the sky were soothing. There was no noise, but the crunch of my boots on the snow. It was the perfect peace my soul needed.

I walked for hours trying to be in the moment, to enjoy the scenery. My phone was on do not disturb (which it was never on before), my heart was heavy, and my mind was tangled. But I was holding onto every step I was taking so that I wouldn't fall in my valley of darkness.

At some point, the path fell into the shadow of trees that arched over my head. It was colder, but the sun shone through the branches and fell on my face.

I stopped, closed my eyes, and allowed myself to feel.

Of course, my Monster started whispering my deepest fears:

- "You are no one."
- "Your friend was right to walk away."
- "They will all do that soon."
- "You're delusional."
- "She never loved who you are."
- "She doesn't care that you aren't her friend anymore."
- "She doesn't miss you."

Those were common thoughts back then, spiraling into my mind at any time of day and night.

I was a Monster in my own eyes and I couldn't see myself differently.

I had become my inside Monster and my most disturbing thoughts.

But in that moment, with the sun on my face and coldness surrounding me, I said no.

I wanted to drive my bus into the light and stay in the peace I had almost found walking in the snow.

So, I told my Monster to get to the back of the bus.

I raised my shaky hand and shone light into its eyes.

I stopped the thoughts by saying "No. Not now. Right now, I'm focusing on that sun on my face and the silence around me."

It was the first time I loved myself just enough not to believe the bullshit I was telling myself.

It was the first time I drove my bus instead of crashing into a wall of self-deprecation.

It was the first time I could stop my cycle of self-loathing.

Since then, those thoughts came and left, and new words replaced the harsh words I used to tell myself. Through the practice of meditation and routines, I've learned other ways to push my Monster away. I will share these with you in next chapter. But for the moment, just raise your hand, shine that light at your Monster, and say, "No. Not right now."

I'm not going to lie, that first step is the hardest.

It's the hardest because changing the narrative about

yourself is the toughest thing you can do. It means accepting that you have a part in what you think of yourself. It means accepting that you have been treating yourself like a piece of shit under your own shoe. It means accepting that you are your own executioner.

That's why changing those negative things you have believed to be true for years and trying to see the positive in you, is painful.

But, the moment you see that how you treat yourself is not okay, the moment you realize that you are the first one to believe your own thoughts and give them power, it will get easier.

HERE ARE SOME HARD TRUTHS I HAVE LEARNED walking in the snow for hours:

- No one can make you believe you're awesome but you.
- No one can be a better best friend to yourself than you.
- No one can step into the light for you.
- No one is coming to save you.
- No one is coming to defend you.
- No one is coming to stop the voices in your head but you.

And that's why this is the hardest step to take, but also the most rewarding.

Gabrielle G.

Therapy

* * *

It takes a lot of courage to say out loud
Things you've been whispering to
yourself
So, know that whatever you feel, I'm
proud
Of you for voicing all the pain you
withheld

Excerpt from Melancholy & Cinnamon
by Gabrielle G.

Exercise 3: Text your best friend

For this chapter, I want you to pretend text your best friend, sister, whoever you are the closest to.

Take your phone and compose the worst text ever in your notes app.

Start with, "I think you are..." and say all the awful things you are thinking about yourself as if you were talking about that person you cherish. Write it all. Anything negative, disgusting, heartbreaking, or shameful that you think about yourself, or that you believe others think about you.

Mine would have been, "I think you are the

worst friend ever. I think you treat people like shit. I think you use people and that you are a fake. That's why no one loves you. That's why you'll die alone. That's why everyone would be better off if you were dead."

Is yours worse? Go on... write whatever you hate about yourself and believe to be true.

All of it. Go for it. Let it out of you.

Then, take a step back. Read it out loud and feel every word.

How do you think your friend would feel if they received that text?

How hurt would they be? How heartbroken would they feel?

Think about how you are feeling right now.

Repeat those words out loud once more. Let them become proof that you are treating yourself horribly and that this needs to change.

Then, take your journal and write how you think your friend would feel if you were to send this text to them.

Take your time. Don't say how bad you would be if you were to send the text, that's not the point here. Focus on how your friend would feel. It doesn't have to be long, but it needs to be truthful. Compare how you think your friend would feel to how you feel writing this text about yourself.

Go back to the text you will never send and

erase it word by word with the intention to see yourself differently.

Once you are done, take a big breath and look at the blank text. Release it all.

Take another breath and relax to prepare yourself for what is next.

Now it's time to compose a text to yourself. A real one this time that you will send to your own number.

In this text, I want you to say all the marvelous things you want to say about your best friend, sister, or whoever you are closest to.

"You're compassionate, you're loving, you're funny, you're amazing..."

Go on... Again, this doesn't have to be lengthy as long as it is truthful.

Once you are done, don't send your text. Not yet.

First, go back to your journal and write about how you feel thinking those things about this person you love. I'm pretty sure that these thoughts will put a smile on your face.

Write it down. Hold on to that feeling.

Now, write all those beautiful things you wrote about your friend in your journal, but this time end each sentence with, "and so am I."

For example, "You are a wonderful person with a compassionate heart, and so am I."

Even if you don't think this about yourself yet, do it.

Think of your friend receiving the text filled with compliments about them and stay in that good feeling. You are doing something good, and now while you are writing in your journal, or the notes app on your phone, you are doing something good **for you**.

Once you're done, read it out loud for yourself to hear.

Read it another time.

Read it again.

Again.

Close your eyes and feel the joy of love fill your heart.

Feel peace embracing you.

Feel light surrounding you.

Take a big breath and stay in this energy as long as you want, or as long as you can stand it.

Release all the darkness you carried for way too long.

If negative thoughts jump in, raise your hand and push them to the back of the bus. Choose you.

Once you are ready, open your eyes. Stay in the light.

Send yourself that amazing, loving text, and

read it. Your new best friend just told you all the amazing things they think about you.

Keep this text on your phone, and don't hesitate to come back to it whenever you need to.

And now, go reward yourself the way you like to, because congratulations are in order!

You just won your first battle against your Monster. You shone the light of love in his eyes and made it silent. It doesn't matter if it was quiet for a minute or for hours. I'm proud of you.

But remember, the battle is not over. So go rest, take your time to master raising your hand to shine that light on the Monster while driving your bus. Do it often. Believe in the good in you.

Don't rush the process; I'll be here when you're ready.

Unworthiness

* * *

Through the cracks of my scars
The whispers became louder
So I listened, to them

They sang lies I believed
About my worst nightmare
So I blindly, joined them

Their cruelty stabbed my heart
With mockery and laughter
But nonetheless I, helped them

In choking my sanity
To kill all that mattered
And chanting my requiem, with them

Excerpt from *Melancholy & Cinnamon* by Gabrielle G.

Chapter 4

Stopping Your Monster

Choose Yourself

It's the days I don't choose myself
That darkness embraces my soul
And feeds a Monster that only grows
To fill what silence has destroyed.

Gabrielle G.

Confession: Even after everything I went through, after having fought darkness, self-deprecation and self-loathing, there are still moments when I don't choose myself.

There are still decisions I make knowing they will pinch my heart in a drawer of regrets, and nevertheless, I deliberately choose to do so.

It hurts less than it used to, and I regret the decision not to choose myself five seconds after, but it still hurts me.. It's like a sting for my ego, something that feeds the Monster inside of me, an instant of weakness that could let the old me reappear.

Even so, I still do it. It's like knowing that eating that donut will make you feel bloated, but you bite into it anyway.

But I don't dwell on it for too long. I have learned to forgive myself for these moments of weakness and to move on.

Yes, it hurts, and I let it hurt, but I allow my mistake to be a reminder of everything I don't want to feel anymore, everything I don't want to be anymore: pain, guilt, heartbreak, shame.

Because, I am laughter and joy and an abundance of love.

I am smiles that warm the tips of fingers and kisses that can bring tingles to the toes.

I am hugs that never end and wrestling on a beach.

I am peace of mind and calmness of heart.

And anytime I don't choose me, I am reminded of what I am not anymore.

Maybe that's why I still make the "bad" decision sometimes...

Maybe that's why I give the Monster scraps of the skins I shed, to remind myself of how much I've changed and to feel grateful that I did.

So, what's my secret?

Well, there is a difference between giving scraps to the Monster and feeding it a whole meal. I used to give him my whole mind and body to feed on, but step by step

I stopped. So, I try to remember that even on days when I feed him scraps, I am okay. I am okay because never making mistakes, being too much in control, not allowing yourself to feel, is the most common mistake you can make in killing the Monster. No one is strong enough to keep going without ever taking a step back, no one is ever fully healed, no one ever has all their shit together. And by never feeding your Monster scraps, you make it so hungry that the day you make one mistake, the day you are too tired to control everything down to the last dot, your Monster feasts and eats you alive. Starving your Monster will only make it bigger, and ignoring it will only make it louder. To kill the Monster, you need to acknowledge where the pain comes from, you need to know why you allow it to whisper those things into your soul, you need to feel what the Monster is trying to tell you.

For a long time (thirty years or so), I pushed the Monster away.

I stopped feeding him altogether, I decided I was stronger than him, and I knew what was best for me. I was cutthroat with it, and I refused to feel anything about it. I knew I hadn't dealt with a lot of things, but I was okay, living in the belief that I had it all sorted out. I believed that if I pushed through, if I didn't feel, if I didn't give in to those thoughts and fears, I was strong.

Breaking news: I wasn't, and I was totally wrong.

In fact, I was just making it worse.

I was making my Monster stronger for the day we would start our war. All the things that I didn't want to feel, that I didn't allow to come to the surface, that I didn't want to address were gaining in strength and waiting to eat me alive.

That's the thing no one tells you: your Monster is a patient beast. It knows it will get you, and it has all the time in the world to do so. It lurks in your shadow laughing at you. You think that you are controlling the monster when, really, it controls every one of your thoughts and every step you take.

It controls your narrative and leads you into darkness one step at the time.

This Monster is sneaky, so sneaky that you might not even know it's in you.

The only way to know if your Monster is around is to acknowledge your fears.

So, tell me, when is the last time you were fearful?

Think about it... What are you afraid of?

I used to be afraid of everything. I was strong and I was always moving forward, but I had those fears that I hid under, things I didn't like to do such a driving, paddling, staying in silence, flying... Though some of my fears were truly there to protect me, such as my fear of jumping off a cliff, others were my Monster controlling me. And, I didn't know! I thought I was such a powerful queen with strong opinions about what I liked and didn't like.

But do you know what makes a queen truly powerful? The awareness she has of her own fears. The awareness of what she needs to work on. The awareness of the Monster trying to eat her from inside.

Not having fears isn't a powerful trait; it is, in fact, a dangerous one.

Being aware of your fears and embracing them nonetheless, that is true power.

So yes...I was afraid. Sometimes I still am. We all have fears. We all have things we need to work on. We all have insecurities. We all have weaknesses, and we should all accept them.

One of my biggest fears was driving. It had become the epitome of my inability to be free. I had heard that I was so clumsy that I wouldn't be able to be a good driver.

I was consumed by the image my whole family had of me as this stupid, insecure teenager who had lived in chaos since birth, and who had so much trouble with distance and space that her body was covered by bruises.

Driving became something I was afraid of, and I let that fear feed my Monster for years. Yes, I had my driving license, but I didn't drive until I was twenty-nine years old. I took more lessons before moving to North America and hated it even more. I always said I hated it. That was my narrative.

Truth is, I was scared to death. Even now, I don't feel comfortable when I drive with another adult next to me. I am afraid they will judge me and say I am doing it wrong. I have stopped myself from going places because I had to drive with someone. Everyone around me knows that if we are to go anywhere together, they are driving.

Nonetheless through the years, I've learned to love driving alone.

Am I the best driver in the world? Not at all. But am I

too fearful to drive anymore? Not really. I detached of what people thought about me. I've stopped saying that I don't like to drive, when in fact I like being alone in a car and feeling free.

But for a long time, I allowed the fear of people being right about my inability, the fear of driving badly and feeling inept, to paralyze me. I kept feeding my Monster and stopped driving altogether for ten years. I let my Monster win and control me until I found the source of the fear—my issue with what people think of me— and could start working on it.

After a summer in the alps where my older sister relentlessly made fun of me for walking in cow poo (I was ten, she was twelve years older), I internalized that nature wasn't my friend. Nature was disgusting and hated me.

Nature was silence and mocking. Nature was everything I hated. Don't get me wrong, the beat of the streets of Paris, London, or New York City runs in my veins, but in the past years, once I let go of the voices of other people, once I accepted that silence was necessary to heal, once nature screamed at me to come and find myself in hikes through woods and up mountain tops, I found peace.

I stopped fearing being seen as ridiculous for walking in poo and worrying what people would think of me, the well-known city girl, embracing nature, and I jumped into this new facet of me. Nonetheless, paddling in a canoe terrified me because I knew I could fall in the water and made fun of. Sooo, I said I didn't like it, and I didn't ever canoe until last summer. When I did, I didn't feel fully confident, but I enjoyed the feeling of freedom it brought me and knowing that my Monster wasn't holding me back anymore. I was taking control. I was paddling, I was climbing mountain, I was driving... In a way, I was free.

People will tell you to grow up, that you need to leave your fear behind and do the thing. It's true, but it's not that easy to do. Because doing the things that scare you without thinking about why they scare you will not kill your Monster. It will only make it stronger in another area of your life. I proved this with my love addiction, over and over. I loved hard and unconditionally to shut up the voices telling me I was unlovable. But in return, I got rejected, and it allowed my Monster to feed on my fear of abandonment. Nonetheless, the next time, I loved harder and gave even more. And, well, you can imagine how that went. It wasn't pretty...

But here is the thing. The only way to fight fear is with love. I'm not the first one to say so, and I won't be the last. But I still want to insist on this.

You need to fight fears, not with the love you crave from others, but with the love you bring to yourself. That's why it's so important you learn to love yourself, because the more you love yourself, the more your Monster will quiet down, the more your fears will become smaller, the more you will shine into this world.

We often let the Monster win because it's easier, because we don't know better, because that's how we think we are, because we believe that it's too late to change, to make a difference, to be different. But tell me, are we supposed to stay the same until we die?

I remember a friend of mine telling me, "That's how I am; I won't change."

How sad is that? You are telling me that when we cross path again in two, five, or ten years, you will be exactly the same person you were the last time we spoke? You won't have tried to evolve, to understand yourself better, to blossom into something else?

We all change.

We are all supposed to change.

And we all have the opportunity to change. All we need is to take that opportunity, and to try to change for the better, not the worse.

Never forget this. This is the starting block of all stories. Whatever your situation or conditions, you can change. The change starts from within and doesn't cost anything. It's as simple as raising our hand and saying, "not for now." It's as simple as looking at ourselves in the mirror, it's as simple as finding compassion for ourselves.

Letting the Monster win is just a habit you picked up along the way in your journey, because some traumas haven't been addressed, because the work hasn't been done, because the light of love hasn't shone your own worth yet.

Not yet, but it will...

We saw in earlier chapters that changing your narrative is difficult. But it's the only way you can bring yourself to drink the cup of self-love.

When I feel unsettled, when I don't choose myself,

when my Monster tells me stories from the point of view of fear and wakes up all my little demons, or when I fall into judging others harshly, I take a big breath, hold my breath for the count of three, exhale and simply say, "Thank you for showing me how I don't want to feel. I recognize what you are saying, and I will address it in due time, but I do not believe any of it. I am love. I am light and, therefore, I am fearless."

The only way to kill your Monster is by inviting in light and love and refocusing your thoughts, your perspective, yourself. You need to realize the way your Monster is making you feel, and you need to **choose** not to feel that way, while still allowing your feelings to go through you more than muffling them.

That's how you kill the beast.

That's how you choose you.

That's how you learn to love yourself.

Your Monster will try to react. It will do anything to survive, anything to take back control. It will give you excuses you will believe. It will tell you that you didn't stop long enough at the stop sign and could kill someone. It will tell you that you don't know how to survive in the wild. It will tell you the lake is filled with disgusting things you can't see if you fall in the water.

It's easy to let the Monster take over, but you have to rise above. You have to do it for you.

"But if I hadn't acted this way, they wouldn't have walked away."

"But if I had been calmer, I would have handled the situation in a better way."

"But if…"

"But if…"

"But if…"

How about leaving that "but" out of your vocabulary for a week or so?

There is no extended exercise or journaling for this chapter, only one small thing to do over and over.

When you feel you are being controlled by your Monster, take a step back, like we did with the bus. But instead of pushing it away, recognize the pattern. Analyze how the Monster makes you feel. Get out of your body, out of your head, and analyze what is going on. Feel the pain, the fear, the shame, the guilt. Don't blame anyone, not even yourself. Don't push any feelings away.

Just pause.

No one is making you feel guilty but your own Monster.

No one is hurting you but your own Monster.

No one is feeding the Monster but you.

So, take a step back and feel it, let it all go through you.

Realign yourself.

Recalibrate your self-love compass, and sternly tell yourself:

"Thank you for showing me how I don't want to feel. I recognize what you are saying, and I will address it in due time, but I do not believe any of it.

I am love. I am light and, therefore, I am fearless."

And, commit to choosing you. Over and over.

Pour yourself a cup of self-love again and again.

If you don't know how to, don't worry. I will explain in the next chapter.

Self-love

* * *

My most beautiful and longest lasting
romance is the one I discovered when
I started to love myself.

Excerpt from To The Man I Loved Too
Much, *by Gabrielle G.*

Chapter 5

Your First Cup of Self Love

For as long as I remember, my sister's ex-husband would say, "To be happy, you have to be selfish," and I struggled for years trying to grasp what he meant. I even found it kind of rude, borderline dickheadish.

He wasn't selfish per se, and for what I knew of him, he wasn't a dickhead. How was it possible that a father, husband, and marketing genius could say something like that? How did it work? I really didn't get it.

Selfish is a big word. It's something we see in a negative light. Something we have been told we should never be.

So how being selfish could make me happy?

I was happy when I thought of others, when I helped them, when...

But was I? Was I really happy helping others, or was I killing myself slowly? Was I really happy doing all this, or was I doing this because I was desperate to be loved?

Twenty years or so later, I have my answer. I wasn't

happy. I was trying to be loved, at any cost. I wasn't authentically helping others, I was expecting love in return, and every time I was failing, feeling alone and hurt. And every time I thought that if next time I helped more, did more, gave more, I would be loved more, too.

How wrong was I?

You've heard it a thousand times, "You can't pour from an empty cup."

I understood the concept, but I truly believed my cup was never empty. Cocky, right?

As a woman, a mother, a small business supporter, a writing entrepreneur, an avid volunteer, I thought that all I needed was a little sleep to get my cup full. That I was like a super tank of love, that I would never run out. I saw this as my happiness, as who I wanted to be, as how I wanted to be seen. I was super woman. I mostly still am, or at least that's what I want to believe, what I was told, what the society showed me and how I thought it should be.

No time to think, no time to stop, if I hustle, I will be happy. Right?

If I take care of others and everything, I will be happy. Right?

If I am in control of everything, I am happy. Right?

So, I became president of the parent's association, raising money for the school, I made sure my kids were educated and smart, I jumped from job to job and one volunteer position to another, I helped anyone who needed help, I wrote for free, I grasped onto anything and everything that brought me value, to everything I believe in: bilingualism, girl's education, women's rights, small business support, climate change, political views... I was helping others change the world, and so I was changing it as well. All of this could only make me happy. I was part of my community, volunteering left and right, helping whoever needed it. I was happy... I should have been happy... Right?

Wrong... Wrong... Wrong...and wrong again.

It took me twenty years to understand what my ex-brother-in-law meant, but once I did, it got me right in the gut.

I remember the day that I understood. I was on a walk, telling a friend that I had been crying in front of my computer daily for weeks, not because I hated my job, but because I didn't get the hit of adrenaline I needed. I didn't feel any joy from my work. I was depressed and I was trying too hard to be loved, to feel worthy, to be...anything.

My friend looked at me with compassion and said, "You're doing too much. I know you think doing a lot is giving you value, but it's killing you...the real you, the one inside your heart, the one you are meant to be."

I didn't say a word. I took every word in and let it go through me.

The next morning when I had to open my computer and start working, her words rang in my brain. I had been trying too hard not to feel. I was doing too much. I was not giving myself worth, instead, I was killing myself.

Not only my cup was empty, but my whole teapot.

I had poured tea onto everyone else's cups and there

was no tea left for me. What's worse is that the ones I poured my tea for had barely even touched it.

To find some joy, I started writing romance on the side. I didn't tell anyone; it was something I was doing for me. I wasn't sure I could do it; I had numerous first chapters of books I had never finished in my computer, and I wasn't going to broadcast my potential failure to anyone. It was a great escape, something I loved doing, something that amused me. It kind of brought me joy... Or, it brought me anxiety with a little joy mixed in. It was a first step.

It was a first step to hell, but back then I didn't know.

I was still lying to myself and not embracing what I really wanted to do because my Monster still had control of everything I did, but I was oblivious to that.

And so, with that first small step, I went back to writing. It was a kind of therapy that I needed at the time, something that was soothing to me... until it fed my Monster even more. But at that moment, it was my first cup of self-love, and I was okay drinking it. Even if it was poisoned by fear.

Nonetheless, without that first cup, I would have never been able to write these words today. I would have never met those who helped me grow. I would have never been able to feel like an imposter, and never started writing poetry to connect to my darkness. I would have never, oh yes, really NEVER, gone to therapy and faced all my traumas. I would have never learned to love-myself and find self-compassion.

So, even if that first cup is now tainted by a story that

had to become darker for me to see the light, that first cup was the most important cup of my journey.

I think that you picking up this book is a good first cup. I know that I cannot change your life, but you can. All I want to do is help you love yourself and realize that pouring and drinking that first cup of self-love isn't that difficult.

In fact, you've already done it.

Maybe you chose to eat something for breakfast that you know makes you feel good, that is not going to make you feel bad in two hours. Or maybe you went on a walk when you felt stressed and overwhelmed instead of being like a hamster in its wheel at your desk. Or maybe you stopped checking the social media of that ex you've had on your mind for weeks now. Or, you did something for you that you haven't done in forever. Or, you decided to start a new project, a new job, a new family.... Anything that you've done FOR YOU counts.

It's a bit like choosing yourself over and over. Every time you choose yourself, you pour a cup of self-love, and so you bring more love into your life and mute your Monster a little more, too.

And, again, choosing you can be as simple as eating fruit instead of chocolate (unless you really want the chocolate!), going for a walk outside, taking a nap when you're tired, or slowing down altogether. It can also be as hard as setting a boundary with someone (more on this later), not internet-stalking an ex, not gossiping, not calling back that friend who drains you, not engaging in a fight you know will bring you nowhere, etc.

Depending on your mental health, on your level of tiredness, on where you are in life, there are millions of things you can do; even having an actual cup of tea in total silence, just to allow yourself to enjoy the peace.

So, what are you going to try?

What are you going to do?

Does it make you feel selfish?

Do you feel like you don't deserve that cup of love?

Do you still believe you are unworthy of loving yourself?

Think about it like needing to pee.

I can go hours needing to pee and not going. But I don't, not anymore. Not only because it's not good for me and it can give me a bladder infection, but because giving yourself the two minutes you need is an act of self-love. It's natural, and it's the most basic form of taking care of yourself, which is self-love.

So, go pee.

I'll wait...

Jokes aside, do you realize how an act of self-love can be so little, but also so necessary?

It may sound kind of silly when I put it like that, but I hope it shows you the way.

Here is a list of the little things and the bigger things I do to fill my cup:

- Shower with a soap that I love the scent of
- Take two minutes extra in the shower to feel good and embrace the light
- Walk in nature as much as I can
- Not answer texts right away
- Read a genre or watch a show I like
- Stop working, reading, or watching TV when I am tired
- Pee when I need to
- Take a big breath when I feel I can't breathe
- Don't look at things I know will hurt my feelings
- Don't look at the social media of people who have that so-called perfect life
- Don't hang out with people who criticize me
- Go to bed early
- Learn new things
- Write whatever I want
- Sing badly and often
- Meditate
- Change my breakfast routine daily
- Do my nails
- Set boundaries with people
- Read self-help books
- Dance
- Eat chocolate daily
- Eat more chocolate
- And then buy chocolate...

THIS LIST IS NON-EXHAUSTIVE AND THERE ARE things I can't share because they're maybe a little too personal. But that's how I pour myself some love, how I choose myself. That's why I am a little more selfish and a lot happier, and that's how I found myself on the path of self-love.

Exercise 4: Dream big. Be selfish.

Time to take your journal and get to work.

As an exercise, I want you to build a reverse ladder.

First, write the biggest, worst, most selfish thing you would like to do that would bring you joy. Dream big. Be awfully selfish.

Mine, for example, is: "Leave everything and everyone and live somewhere between a beach and a mountain where I could write and enjoy walks, beautiful landscapes, and peace."

Then, write why it would be selfish.

For me, that would be selfish because it would mean leaving my family behind (yep, they aren't in that house with me), and it would mean having a totally different life away from my friends. It would be something only for me and no one else.

And then write why it would be your ultimate cup of self-love.

For me: "It would be my ultimate cup of self-love because it would bring me a feeling of accomplishment, peace, and joy, and it's something I've wanted for a long time."

Then, write what could be the step underneath that, something a little less selfish you could do that you would still enjoy. And what's something else a little less selfish, and another one, and another one after that.

List them all until you arrive at the smallest thing you could do for yourself.

And once you have it, you do it.

And, once you've done it, you work on that guilt you might feel. You tell yourself that being happy, even if it's for five minutes because you went pee when you needed to, is not selfish. It's a necessity. It's an act of choosing you. It's an act of self-love. A blanket of self-compassion that you need to wrap yourself into.

And every day, you can add to your ladder, and you can change your mind, and you can do whatever you need and want as long as it makes you happy. This doesn't make you a Monster; it helps quiet yours. And as you find joy in the smallest things you do for yourself, you continue building up your ladder until maybe one day, you get to this biggest, worst, most selfish thing you would like to do. And who knows, maybe by then, you won't find it selfish anymore, and instead you'll find it the purest act of self-love.

I stood on top of fake mountains
And swam upstream rivers of pain
But my heart...still felt empty
I bathed in a freezing lake of truth
And slept away my years of youth
And still felt...desperately lonely
I rode widely on the back of death
Prayed the stars for one last breath
And found my soul...opening slowly
And when light shone on my mistakes
I drank shame's drops to melt my aches
And knew time had come...to love me.

Gabrielle G.

Chapter 6

For Give

I was listening to an audio book or a podcast when a quote hit me. I don't exactly remember what it said, but it was something along the lines of,

"There is no true self-love without self-compassion.

And there can't be self-compassion without forgiveness..."

LET ME REWIND A LITTLE.

For the past twenty years, I've been amazed by the ability of some of my friends to admit that they love themselves. Until not long ago, I didn't get it.

I was sure that I loved myself; yes, I was confident, smart, witty. I loved how I shone, but I was also a little pretentious, kind of elitist, and so judgmental. Nonetheless, I was not the kind to say I loved myself. Never ever. I was filled with too many insecurities to say it out loud. I was afraid that if I said out loud how much I loved myself, everyone would see that I didn't and therefore, no one would really love me.

I wanted to be loved and liked and appreciated by everyone. I wanted to find my next dose of love and get high on how others loved me. Now I know that the self-love I wasn't ready to show was simply an act. I didn't really love myself the way one should love themselves. I didn't love who I was, or who I was becoming.

This cup of self-love was a tough one to drink. My Monster still had control over me then, and was gripping my throat with fears daily. I kept wondering if there would be enough love for my children after I poured myself a cup. Or if I would be able to still love the love of my life or my family after I poured love into my own cup...

It was a disaster. I felt like I was spilling self-love all around my cup, making a disaster of my relationships, choosing me in all the wrong ways, and victimizing myself when I should have been putting myself on a pedestal. I felt the world was against me, I took that friend who I have spoken about in previous chapters and decided she was against me as well as all the friends we had in common. I vomited words of pain and sadness, and under the pretext of choosing me, I distanced myself from people I didn't feel had my back hundred percent. I lost many friends and cut many relationships during that time because I wasn't used to bringing myself love, and I was clumsy and quivering in my delivery.

As I said before, it was a mess. Well, I was a mess, and I felt like I kept cleaning up after myself, apologizing all the time for all my unpracticed actions and words, only to keep missing my cup each time I poured. I felt empty to the core. I was an addict with shaky hands missing my dose. And unless I started looking at myself thoughtfully and sincerely, nothing would change. My cup would still be empty, and I would become even more isolated by messing up every relationship I had.

The change came the day that, after having drunk a little too much because I wanted to numb the feelings of loneliness and unworthiness I felt, I told my teenager who had been battling with depressive and suicidal thoughts that she would never be happy.

That kid had been my everything since her birth. She was the dose of unconditional love that saved me from feeling unworthy. She was a good kid (still is), a smart, beautiful angel, and here I was one of her biggest insecurities in her face because I couldn't deal with people walking away from me. What the heck was I doing?

The next day, filled with guilt, remorse, shame, and all the other emotions I couldn't bear, I apologized and tried to make it better.

As the daughter of an alcoholic, I have lived through way too many apologies to know that an apology without a changed behavior means nothing at all.

Even though I was not an alcoholic, and my addiction has never been alcohol, I didn't like who I was anymore after a few glasses. As I had always hated this idea that mothers need a glass of wine to unwind, and that alcohol makes you cool, it was one of the easiest decision I took in my journey.

Still, I knew alcohol wasn't the addiction I needed to fight. The real addiction was the one I missed the hit for: love.

As every step-based recovery program begins, I first recognized my own toxicity. I admitted I was powerless and that my life had become unmanageable. I was lost and I needed guidance. I was at the end of the road, and I needed to stop the vicious cycle I had fallen into. So, after looking at myself deeply in the mirror, I took a big breath and decided, right there, that I was done drinking, I was done finding excuses, and I was done self-sabotaging because of my fears and my lack of self-love.

I went deep inside of me and started a healing journey that scared me to death but was more than necessary. I was like an explorer, diving into myself. I spent hours swimming down into the depths of who I was and who I wanted to be.

I would sit outside on my front porch and just...*feel*, trying to understand myself, taking in whatever was happening around me, and attempting to see why I was triggered and what was triggering me, why I felt so lost without some people in my life, why I loved this person so much or that one too little.

In fact, I wanted to know what those months of depression were about.

Some call it shadow work, others call it exploring

your dark side, some say it's focusing on yourself; I call it "whying" yourself.

For me, this was the hardest, most frightening thing I could do, and the most courageous thing, too. I was facing my demons, my Monster, my ego, and my fears. I was asking why relentlessly until I found the reasons behind my actions and the root of my problems.

WHY DID THAT PERSON BOTHER ME SO MUCH?
   Why did that man attract me so much?
   Why did I feel drawn to chaotic relationships?
   Why did I feel so alone?
   Why did I feel different?

AS I ANSWERED THESE QUESTIONS, I JOURNALED OR wrote poems about them and let everything out. And sometimes when I needed to, I cried, I hugged myself, and I let myself breathe.

Rooted

* * *

My roots were tangled in traumas of my
     childhood
So, I took a comb and patiently worked
     my way through

Gabrielle G.

It hurt like a bitch but made me good,
To heal the wounds of how I grew.

Excerpt from Melancholy & Cinnamon
by Gabrielle G.

MOST OF ALL, I CAME TO UNDERSTAND MYSELF, because by "whying myself," I opened the door to self-compassion.

I gave myself the opportunity to self-explain, to be self-understood.

It is important to see that I wrote the chapter title as FOR-GIVE. Forgiveness for others and whatever you think they did to wrong you, hurt you, or destroy you, can't come to fruition if you don't first forgive yourself. And, to forgive yourself, you need to give yourself some self-love and self-compassion.

Forgiving yourself for your shortcomings, the words you told others, your actions, the life you created, the way you treated yourself, the thoughts you have about your-self, the people you hurt, for anything you have done, is how you can save your own life. Of course, you need to change your behavior afterwards—I just told you how I did that—but forgiving yourself is the first step. Because if you go into this shadow work without any forgiveness for yourself, all you will do is spiral even more into self-depreciation. It's never too late to start...

Now that I can look back to that time, I realize that the way I communicated was needy but cold, and people took my act of self-love as a direct attack. I apologized to some. Others showed me they didn't care either way. To move on, I had to forgive myself. As the song by Rag'n'Bone Man says, "I'm only human after all..." Same with my daughter, I victimized myself until I was ready to destroy one of the most important relation in my life, I changed my behavior, asked for forgiveness, forgave myself and moved forward.

To move forward, you need to give yourself a break. You need to understand that you are just human after all. You need to find your self-compassion and believe that you deserve it.

Please trust me, someone who has been filled with guilt and shame most of her life when I tell you that you deserve to give yourself a break.

Exercise 5: Forgiving yourself

To help you do so, I created the next exercise. It is based on the Hawaiian Ho'oponopono, a forgiveness song, but adapted for this chapter. This Ho'oponopono forgiveness song was an amazing step in my journey. There are free guided meditations for the traditional version on

YouTube. Don't hesitate to find and follow one of them in addition to doing this exercise

Read the meditation below a few times or record it, and then close your eyes and play it back.

Take a big breath, release it in a huge sigh.

Take another breath and release again.

Start breathing slowly but deeply at a rhythm that is comfortable for you.

Find calmness. Focus on your breath.

Call upon the positive side of you. Imagine you are facing yourself.

Find your own eyes. Look at yourself and smile.

Take another deep breath and release it.

Imagine taking the hands of the positive side of you while still looking into your own eyes.

Smile some more.

Breathe gently and slowly say:

"I'm sorry.

Please forgive me.

I love you."

Let go of what is in your heart and repeat it again...

"I'm sorry.

Please forgive me.

I love you."

Take your time, there is no rush...

Repeat it once more.

"I'm sorry.

Please forgive me.

I love you."

See yourself smiling.

Feel the light, the love entering your heart and the burden of guilt and shame lifting.

Let go of the hands of the positive side of you, thank them for their time. Thank yourself for giving yourself the time for this exercise.

Return to your breath. Slowly breathe and let the light surround you.

When you are ready, open your eyes.

Now, I would like you to repeat each of the sentences below out loud, with a hand on your heart. Believe that this is the positive side of you responding to your apology.

"I forgive myself for the ways I've hurt myself through action or inaction."

"I know I've acted out of fear, pain, and confusion, and for today, I offer myself forgiveness."

"I forgive myself."

Now, be proud of your work. Repeat it with pride and love. Congratulate yourself. Let your past mistakes go. Breathe.

I'm proud of you.

In a perfect world, doing this work on yourself should be enough to let you live happily ever after. Unfortunately, it's usually not.

Once you have worked on yourself, once you've seen your shortcomings and your mistakes, and found the root of the problem, if you feel that self-forgiveness isn't enough, I encourage you to reach out to some people you might have hurt in the past. But—and this is a big BUT—do so only if you have no expectations in return. Don't reach out and apologize if you want anything from the person in return. If you have any expectations of rekindling a relationship, of forgiveness, closure, redemption, or anything else, you might get disappointed, hurt, find reasons to self-deprecate, and end up letting your Monster out again.

It is important to be able to understand this to really apologize from the heart and for yourself.

In fact, I want to tell you something that changed the way I think:

You don't need closure to be forgiven.

You don't need anyone to give you their words to be forgiven.

You can do the same exercise we just did and replace yourself with the person you hurt. You can ask forgiveness this way, and believe that, in a way, they will receive your apology, and that, for the moment, it is enough for you to continue on your path. And maybe one day you will be ready to step forward and talk with them directly.

Apologies

* * *

The path to unconditional love
The path to peace
The path to forgiveness
But I keep forgetting
Some people never want to be truly happy
But that's not me...
Not anymore
Therefore, I am sorry...

Gabrielle G.

I STARTED THE YEAR WITH TAKING RESPONSIBILITY and making amends by apologizing to a few people, and it felt amazing. It helped me turn the page without needing any more closure.

Whether or not the people I apologized to believed me was none of my business.

I had changed so much in such little time, no one really knew who I had become except the people who had been by my side on my journey, and the new friends who I met along the way.

The same goes for forgiving others.

You don't need to talk to someone, to reopen the door to a relationship, to have a big talk with someone who hurt you in order to forgive them.

Forgiveness is never for the other person; it is ALWAYS for us.

Forgiveness is the only closure your heart and soul need. The rest is only ego. The apology you want is a tactic from your Monster to keep you out of the love and the light that your soul needs to evolve. The apology is only something you want to prove you were right. And let's be honest, if you were right, you already know so. You don't need an apology from anyone. What you need is compassion for the person who has lost your trust, your love, or whatever you removed. You need to forgive so you can stop feeding your Monster. You need to forgive so you can grow. You need to forgive so you shine.

Exercise 6: Forgiving others

Here is a journaling exercise followed by a visualization practice that should help you forgive others and set yourself free.

Take your journal and free write about a

situation where someone hurt you. Tell what happened to you, who hurt you, and what feelings are lingering inside of you because of the situation. Let it all go on paper.

Then write about why you couldn't forgive until now, what you needed from the other person and why.

Go into the details.

Then, think, how would your life be if you could forgive this person?

Write it all down.

Would forgiving them help you?

Would you feel lighter?

Would you be a better person?

How would it change you?

Once you're done, put your pen down and read what you wrote.

Take a big breath in and release it.

Do so as many times as you need to.

When you feel you are ready, write a list of forgiveness.

Begin your list with, " Dear XXX, I forgive you."

Then, start listing whatever burdens you've been carrying from this situation, whatever burdens you need to be free of.

Let it all out on paper; your list can include the smallest things and the biggest.

Here is mine as an example:

Dear You, I forgive you.

I forgive you for making me feel small.

I forgive you for thinking I didn't trust you and hurting me in the process.

I forgive you for not protecting me when I needed it the most.

I forgive you for choosing them over me when you kept telling me I was more.

I forgive you for being stubborn in your silence.

I forgive you for not believing me.

I forgive you for thinking you could be happy without me and trying to be.

I forgive you for not following up on your promise to defend our connection.

I forgive you for not understanding my distress and choosing peace over my chaos.

I forgive you for walking away.

I forgive you for the tears I shed and the pain you inflicted on me.

I forgive you for not liking cheese and not always understanding my sense of humor.

I forgive you for loving others more than you loved us.

I forgive you for connecting with those who have hurt me.

I forgive you for not hearing my apology.

I forgive you for not wanting to know me again.

I FORGIVE YOU.

Your turn now...

Once all is written and released, close your eyes and let it all go with a deep sigh.

Take another breath, thinking about forgiveness and release it all.

Start breathing slowly but deeply at a rhythm that is comfortable for you.

Find calmness. Focus on your breath.

Imagine you are facing the person you need to forgive. Find their eyes. Look at them. Let the emotions go through you.

Take another deep breath and release it.

Breathe gently and slowly say:

"I forgive you for the ways you have hurt me through action or inaction."

"I might not understand why you acted that way, but I won't be held hostage by your actions. I won't live in anger, pain, or confusion, and so today, I offer you my forgiveness."

"I forgive you."

"I forgive you."

"I. Forgive. You. And I let you go."

Breathe. Feel the light, the love entering your heart and the burden of this story lifting off your heart.

Return to your breath, and when you are ready, open your eyes. And be ready to let go...

Forgiveness doesn't come easy. It took me many attempts and a lot of asking the Universe for help to go through it.

Repeat this exercise as often as you need.

Love yourself. Forgive yourself. Apologize if you need to. Forgive others, and most importantly, set yourself free.

Breathe

Close your eyes

Feel the wind on your face

Deploy your wings

Take the leap of faith

Free fall

Let go

Be free

And finally fly

This is a new beginning

Not an old ending

So, trust me when I say

Jump

Gabrielle G.

Chapter 7

Clean Up Your Mess

Warning: this is a chapter of unshaved legs and
unwashed faces...

I t's with the littlest, smallest, self-negligence acts we
do daily that we disrespect ourselves the most. I realized that the hard way, over time.

At my lowest in my self-love journey, I couldn't find
the strength to shave my legs or clean my face. I still took
a shower every morning because I can't stand not to wash
my hair daily, but my other self-care acts were falling
behind.

What was the point of taking care of myself when I
felt I was an ugly old fat cow? Adding zits to my face and
hair on my legs was just the continuity I needed.

I became so obsessed with healing my wounds and

doing the work on a spiritual level that I was neglecting the physical level, and becoming kind of a slob.

I worked on the floor, surrounded by an organized mess. I let candle wax drip off furniture and recycling go overboard. I dressed like shit most of the time, just sliding on a way-too-big pair of jeans and a T-shirt I barely looked at.

I judged myself daily, allowing my Monster to feed on my shame about the care I couldn't provide to myself, and went deeper into a pit of self-deprecation with every step I took toward healing. I was working on myself and letting myself go at the same time, as if I didn't have the energy to do it all.

Again, I felt like a fraud, and so again the Monster woke up:

"No wonder no one could love me with smudged mascara and hairy legs."

"No wonder I was such a mess when everything around me was falling apart."

"No wonder I was so unworthy of love when I couldn't even take care of myself properly."

It was not a good look, and it was not a healthy way to live.

Even though I had started to love myself and done the bare minimum of peeing when I needed to and choosing myself over some unhealthy relationships, I still wasn't there yet. I still couldn't fully take care of me. It was as if I couldn't take the next step, a step that seemed so futile, but also oh so important in my self-love journey.

Be brave enough to start over
To create the life you want
To chase your dreams wherever they
*   lead you*
And while you do so,
Embrace yourself
Because you are in the driver's seat
Of the rest of your life.

Gabrielle G.

AS BOSS-BABES, MOTHERS, WIVES, SISTERS, AND ALL that we can be, caring for ourselves is a step we simply forget. We are so tangled up with worry about what we should do, how we should be, and what we have to provide, that we sometimes don't have the energy to clean up our own mess.

I am not only talking about cleaning the mugs that lie next to your bed and the wad of receipts in your purse, but washing your face, putting the cap back on your cream, putting away your laundry, reorganizing your books, doing your nails, getting your hair cut, etc. I am speaking about anything that makes you feel lighter, cleaner, and more in tune with your soul, your body, and your physical surroundings.

This step was another hard one for me. Even as I write this chapter, I think I need to shave my legs again and clean up some of my mess on the floor of my office.

It's the one cycle I can't totally break. I am still kind of ashamed of it sometimes, and I work on it constantly.

The thing is, I never did those things for me. I shaved my legs in winter only when I had a boyfriend or a skirt to wear, and I cleaned my house only because I was told to, and because the mess bothered other people more than me. I always lived in chaos and never, never took care of myself for my own good.

And so, every time I fall a little behind in the self-love department, that is the first thing that goes away. That's how I know I need to make the extra effort to get back on track and to be mindful of my own self-care.

Over the years, I have discovered that the best way to keep up with my self-care is to make it a routine and try to stick to it.

Like children, adults crave routine. Especially in the self-care game. I have made a point to do the same things, in the same order, daily and within an hour.

At the beginning it was hard, I generally hate routines and the idea of doing the same things in the same order every day just for myself seemed like torture.

Which, it wasn't. Let's be clear... Taking a nice bath, painting my nails, washing my face, moisturizing, cleaning my favorite room where I spent most of my days, was the bare minimum I could do for myself...but the idea of actually doing it seemed insurmountable.

So, I wrote the routine down in my phone notes. I would force myself to book some time in my calendar and do it. I did so every day or every week, every two weeks, twice a week, whatever and whenever I needed it. And slowly, this became a normal thing I did for me, and then without me realizing it, it was a habit I couldn't live without.

I do the same with every new habit I want to implement: exercising, going to the gym, walking, doing yoga, cooking, reading... You can do the same for whatever you need to become a routine.

The mental mess followed.... Who would have thought having smooth legs would clear my mental fog? But it did because it removed a huge part of the burdens my Monster was feeding on.

Same with what I ate, what I did, what I watched, what I read. Step by step, the shift occurred. By washing my face and shaving my legs, I showed my Monster that I was my own priority. That I was fighting back. That I was stronger than it thought. One small step, one small little thing can change the perspective you have on your own life, on who you are, on your own power.

Because, that's what washing your face and cleaning your mess does...it empowers you. It gives you back the power of the queen or king you are. It shows your Monster that you do have your shit together after all, and it makes the Monster shrink smaller, and smaller, and smaller, because the routine is not something that will go away easily...

And, when you feel like you don't want to comply with your self-imposed routine, listen to your inner mama. Listen to that voice that nags you because it wants the best for you. Listen to this little voice that wants good things to happen to you and for you, and comply with what you know is the best for you. If you want to skip washing your face, do... but remember how it is going to make you feel tomorrow.

Mothering ourselves is a higher step than best-friending ourselves, because, ideally, a mother's love is unconditional. And that is the goal here, to love ourselves unconditionally, so that we don't need anyone else to love us. Even if your mother wasn't that kind of mom, you have seen enough movies and read enough books to know what I am talking about.

Hug your inner child, hug your soul, do what is best for you, stick to the routine you created for yourself, shave your legs and wash your face.

I hope you understand now that the leg shaving and face washing are just examples. Do whatever you need to do to continue pouring cups of love into your own soul. We tend to forget to choose ourselves, over, and over, and following this routine is choosing yourself, again and again, every day, until it's not even a second thought, until it becomes part of who you are, until you can feel safe with yourself, until you can feel your own love just by putting moisturizer on your face, until you feel you don't need to choose you, because you know you ARE choosing you...without any doubts.

Exercise 7: Create your routine

Here is how you can create your own routine:

Decide what routine you need. Is it more exercise, better self-care, or meditation? Journal about what it is you need to give yourself more love.

Set small goals. Start with one small thing. One small step at a time, and add on once you're ready. For example, don't start with exercising for one hour daily; fifteen minutes is enough if you haven't moved in years.

Write down your steps, or buy what you need to buy, or research what you need to research.

Be consistent. Same time, same day, same steps.

Make it fun! It will bring you so much more joy and will make you love yourself faster.

Track your progress! Yes, at the beginning write down your streak. Motivate yourself.

Reward yourself. Please do! It's the most important step. Buy yourself little things, make yourself your favorite meal, get flowers etc.

Once you've started your routine, write about it in your journal, "Today I started my routine and I feel..." And whatever you feel, adjust the routine until you feel only joy and love when you are following it.

A self-love, self-care, self-routine must be something proactive, not reactive. Don't wait to be burnt out, don't wait to be depressed, don't wait to have no energy left before pouring yourself lots of love cups. And of course, refill your cup as much as possible.

Once you have mastered a simple routine, I encourage you to go further in taking care of yourself. When I did, I felt so free, so authentic, so me. It was a feral freedom. This is something we will talk about more later, the freedom of it all, but for the moment, if you are ready to go deeper, read below.

Here are ten steps to go further in your self-care routine.

If it feels wrong, don't do it.

Say *exactly* what you mean.

Trust your instincts.

Never speak badly about yourself.

Don't be afraid to say, "No," when something doesn't sit well with you.

Don't be afraid to say, "Yes," when it scares you.

Be kind to yourself.

Let go of what you can't control and what doesn't serve you anymore.

Stay away from drama and negativity.

CHOOSE YOURSELF WITH EVERY BREATH YOU TAKE.

You can pick and choose one to start with, and stick to it for one week. If, once the week has passed, you don't feel good about how it's going, add another week of the same routine, but tweak it to apply to your own life. Once you've mastered one step, add on another one and practice your expanded routine for another week.

Never forget that you can come back to it.

Never hesitate to change a few things here and there.

Never think it is too hard, or that you can't do it.

You got this! You really do.

Now, close the book, go on a walk, wash your face, or shave your legs.

Do whatever you need to take care of yourself.

Take fifteen minutes.

Don't pick up your phone.

Don't lose precious time doing something you know will make you feel bad.

Choose yourself.

Love yourself.

And then journal about it!

And, in the next chapter, we'll learn to be smart and to do less so we can love ourselves more.

Gabrielle G.

When the world spins
and everything seems lost
take a breath
take a step back
take a minute
and allow yourself to do less
So you can love yourself more
and not burn out
your heart and soul

Gabrielle G.

Chapter 8

Be Smart

Sometimes doing less is attracting more.

It's not what we are used to hearing or what we even want to hear. We have been conditioned to think that by doing a lot and working hard, we will get what we want. We live in a world that never stops. Remember when the city that never sleeps used to be only New York City? Well, now the whole world doesn't sleep, and we can be entertained, or keep our minds occupied 24/7. And by doing so, we avoid self-love, we avoid our problems, we avoid our own thoughts. Life has become a giant distraction that tears us apart from who we really are. And we don't even complain about it because we have been taught that's how we will get our dreams to come true. Even worse, when we do nothing, we feel utterly irresponsible.

When I started writing romance, and therefore my small business as a self-published author, I used to work all the time. I never stopped. I always had something to do, something to learn, something to write. And when I wasn't doing so, I had the kids, the husband, the house, the chores. It never stopped, and I LOVED IT.

I was proud of my productivity, my time management, my organization. I was Wonder Woman, right? And my ego was shining so bright at the idea that I had it all. My Monster was gloating.

But things caught up and my life unraveled. Depression crept in and I learned another lesson in life: doing too much is just another way to not give yourself enough.

Read that again.

Doing too much is just another way to not give yourself enough.

After months of staring at a wall asking myself how I got there, I started to work outside the house again. Mostly because I needed to occupy my mind so I wouldn't spiral for hours.

As I had decided to stop writing romance, there were no books to release every three months, no chapters to write daily, no marketing to push every week, so, I had all the time in the world to replay all my shortcomings. I needed a distraction, but I knew that I mentally didn't have the energy to work a full-time job. Thankfully, as my poetry book had been selling well, I could afford to work only part time and devote the rest of my hours to healing.

What I didn't expect is that the person I worked for would be so awesome about mental health.

On a low mental-health day, my boss realized I was

not in the best head space. She is known to go directly to the point, and so, without any small talk, she looked at me and said, "Remember, this is just a job. This isn't life."

It took me a moment to compute.

This was just a job.

This wasn't life.

I repeated it a few times, trying to scramble the words back together.

She continued, "Try to do less."

The first time I did less, I felt like I was sitting with ants in my pants, in my spine, and in my soul. It was so uncomfortable, and it felt lazy and crazy to not be doing anything.

But then I tried to shift my mindset.

This was a time for me to rest my soul.

This was a time for me to show myself that I loved me.

I needed to spend time doing nothing the same way I needed to grab coffee with my best friend. And, as I was my own best friend, I needed double the time I spent with myself. It didn't mean losing myself in reading, or researching self-help theory, or learning a new skill.

No, it meant doing nothing. No multitasking, no social media, no phone, no distraction. Maybe listening to soft music while I was walking in nature. Or my favorite playlist while I was taking a bath. Or just silence while I was closing my eyes. Just me, my peace, and I, and all the love and kindness I gave to others poured into my own heart.

Try it.

First it will be hell.

Your ego is going to persuade you that the world needs you.

Your Monster is going to wake up the truths you are hiding in your basement. You're going to need to find answers, and you'll want to move and to do things because the laundry can't wait, and the dishwasher needs emptying, and the contract needs to be sent, and the clients need an answer and, and, and...

But let's take a minute and think.

We are not that important.

We are no one but ourselves, and if we can't take some time to do less, to recharge, to put our life on pause while we pour a cup of the most important self-love potion...we will end up being nothing, not even ourselves.

Allowing yourself to do less and to take a step back will help you see everything much clearer than you do now. It will open a new world of possibilities and it will help you know who you truly are, what you truly want, and why you should love yourself more.

There is no better time to start than now, right?

So read the lines below and then put the book down and take five minutes to meditate. Do it for you. Spend time alone with yourself.

This will help you with sitting in stillness during your day-to-day chores.

Choosing to spend five minutes with yourself will help improve everything in your life. From the strength of your brain, to your ability to calm your Monster. It will help you to find peace, and soothe your anxiety, your self-depreciation, your darkness.

Incorporating a five-minute mindfulness meditation practice can become a strong routine to help you in changing your life. And the more you meditate, the more time you spend with yourself, the more you do less, the more you live in the moment.

Exercise 8: Spend time with yourself

Read what follows to yourself or record yourself and listen to it later.

Sit comfortably on a pillow and close your eyes.

Breathe deeply in and release your breath slowly.

Let your breath become steady and guide you to peace.

Slowly say, "My world is on pause, and I am safe."

Breathe in.

Breathe out.

"My world is on pause, and I am safe."

Breathe in.

Breathe out.

"I am doing less, and doing so, I will attract more."

Breathe in.

Breathe out.

"I will attract more abundance. More peace. More productivity. More healing. More of everything."

Breathe in.

Breathe out.

"I will attract everything I need because I know how to take care of myself."

Breathe in.

Breathe out.

"And by doing less, I am showing my Monster that I am putting myself first."

Breathe in.

Breathe out

"I am showing my Monster that I love myself."

Breathe in.

Breathe out.

"I love myself."

Continue with your breathing until you feel calm and centered.

Then open your eyes slowly and thank your-self for this five-minute break.

Do this as many times as you need to during the day. Do it especially when you are feeling stressed, or frantic in your productivity. When you are spiraling in the hamster wheel, stop and let yourself be rocked by the sway of the wheel stopping slowly. It's almost like a hammock, if you think about it...

Take longer breaks on the weekend and go on walks, stop the world around you, and learn not to be productive. Nonetheless, be careful not to distract yourself. You have to be mindful, present, and agree that this is a pause to love yourself more, not an escape to avoid yourself or your thoughts.

The line is thin, and so that you don't cross it, ask yourself if you are showing yourself some self-love or if you are in fact avoiding life. I found that there was a difference for me when I read all the time and wasn't dealing with anything around me, than when I read only a book or three per month and still was present in my life.

There was also a difference when I walked to count my steps (productivity disguised as fitness) and when I walked to enjoy nature and birds chirping (mindful self-care). But all this depends on how we live our life daily.

In order to find your own limits and guidelines, you can write about it in your journal.

Ask yourself, "When does my self-care end and my escapism begin?"

Or you can make two columns. In one, write what you do for just yourself and in the other one write what you do because you're bored or trying to escape the life you have.

I know this is a hard step because it's looking

at yourself in the truth mirror and having open-thought surgery when you were only trying to take a five minutes break for yourself.

But it's the best cup of self-love you can pour. It's the moment that your perception shift. It's the moment you say, "This is not going to work for me anymore," to your Monster, to the bad habits you picked up along the way, to all your insecurities. It's the moment your perception of yourself shifts and when you are finally ready to set boundaries with your entourage, with your family, with yourself.

And it's the moment you are ready to be free.

So, do less, listen to your heart and soul, spend time alone with yourself, bring yourself on dates, eat by yourself in a restaurant, spoil yourself with mindful time, choose you, and set yourself free.

I made lots of mistakes
Not knowing who I was
And burned lots of bridges
Trying to mend my scars
There are no excuses
Only apologies
Remorse from the past

And heartfelt memories
And as I restore myself
Embracing the new me
I can feel darkness' end
'Cause healing set me free

Gabrielle G.

Chapter 9

Boundawhat?

I surround myself with light...
A bright evanescent one that shines over
my thoughts.
A powerful white bubble protecting me
from the darkness some try to cast
upon me.
I cut the cord of discord trying to control
me and mute their laughter to silence.

Gabrielle G.

During my first therapy session, my therapist looked at me dead on and said something about me not having any boundaries. I took offense between my sobs of depression. I was so assertive, so good at telling people what I wanted and how I wanted it to be. I had been a badass bitch for so long. I knew how to say no.

I paused...

Did I know how to set boundaries? Had I been a badass bitch in the past years, or had my anxieties, doubts, and self-loathing taken over who I used to be?

With whom was I clear about my dos and don'ts?

I thought hard, so hard my head hurt.

The only people I was good at setting boundaries with were my kids. With others? Nothing. I would say "whatever," and fold...always fold. Always fold to please, to be loved, not to be abandoned by the people I loved.

The forty-year-old I had become didn't really set boundaries or say what she had on her heart, and she had no idea how to anymore.

I had become a people pleaser, giving a lot, too much, always to be sure that I would be loved, but I never felt loved enough in return.

I did things for external love and not really from self-love anymore.

I kept letting myself down, accepting situations that were hurtful, not saying anything because I was afraid, or when I did say something I wasn't loud enough to heard.

I let people's opinions of me, my work, my life, eat at me. I couldn't tell them to fuck off anymore and felt resentful when they did so to me. It was a free-for-all and I felt invisible, unloved, and misunderstood all the time.

And because I felt this way, I didn't respect others' boundaries either. I was needy, I felt lost, I held on too tight to anyone who showed me a little love. It was the unhealthiest I had been in years.

I didn't understand how boundary violation disrupts relationships. I was lost as my therapist talked to me about the different kinds of boundaries and their differences. I was amazed by how easily I could see myself in some patterns or understand my entourage better after seeing theirs.

I won't explain in details the different types of boundaries, there are a lot of books about them, but I want to give you an analogy to let you peek into the subject.

Try to imagine boundaries as fences around your dream house.

The main four boundaries are enmeshment, codependency, trauma bonding, and counterdependency. Now, let's focus on the fences.

IN AN ENMESHED RELATIONSHIP, THERE IS NO FENCE, or if there is, it's the same fence running through the whole neighborhood, with the exact same wood, same height, and same grass on the other side of it, because individualization is not acceptable. There is no sense of separation between you and your neighbors, and everyone is similar. You spend hours with your neighbors (aka the people you are in relationships with) without any quality, and everyone in the whole neighborhood speaks as if with one voice, saying the exact same things.

In a codependent relationship, we have our own

fence, but we let people break it, over and over. We let them drink on our property and throw their beer cans for us to pick up. And, instead of kicking them out, we help them by finding solutions for their problems and protecting them. We do this so we won't be rejected. We enable behaviors that we know are bad for our own house, but we smile and are just happy the person is here with us.

In trauma bonding you start to believe that your fence being broken is your fault, so you remove it totally, thinking that you were a little crazy to think you needed to put up a fence in the first place. Without the fence, you let others violate your emotional and intellectual space, entering an endless cycle of unhealthy relationships because you don't think you are worthy of more.

With counterdependency, you have a fence soooo high that no one can ever get in; people are kept at a distance. This is the because of the difficulty of being vulnerable, your inability to ask for help, your desire to keep emotional distance at all costs because "you have your boundaries," though it is really because of your fears. Fears of relying on someone else, fears of becoming dependent on others, and, therefore, fears of being abandoned at some point...

Now, let's go back to my therapy session.

There I was, in my mental hell, thinking about boundaries, and what they were, and how I could set them up.

My therapist encouraged me to tell others how I felt. That was the first step, and so I did.

But, you know what happens when you haven't shared how you really feel with people for years, and suddenly you speak up? It's a mess.

When I told people what I really thought and felt, it came out as a storm of emotions, and the results were catastrophic. I should have waited. I should have been more rational, explained better.

To be honest, when I started to get out of my first depressive episode, my life was a disaster.

I was often oversharing, overthinking, overanalyzing, people pleasing, not feeling worthy, wanting to save everyone. I was needy, unsure of myself, and anxious ALL THE TIME. I was so scared to end up alone. I was prideful, too, but I had no voice anymore because every time I spoke up, I was told that it was a ME problem, that I didn't trust people, that I should know that's not what was meant, that I couldn't take a joke, that I was difficult, or too emotional, or just so dramatic.

When it all blew up with my closest friends, with my entourage, with my family, and I ended up alone after the darkest time of my life, I thought I deserved it.

How sad it is to believe you deserve the worst!

Thankfully, I don't think so anymore, because the fence I built, the boundaries I put up, showed me that my house was worth as much as my neighbor's, and that I shouldn't allow anyone to throw bricks at it.

And that's where I want to bring you.

You need to build a fence that protects your peace,

your worth, and your light. Not a wall, not a Swiss cheese fence, not the exact same fence as your neighbors, but a beautiful, unique fence that helps you pour some love into your own self.

The first thing is to speak your truth. Sometimes you don't even need words to do so. A friend of mine felt obligated to post things on social media because they received them for free. In the "Bookstagram" world, it is expected that if you receive a book, a book box, an e-book, or anything for free, you should post it on Instagram and gush about it.

So, this friend didn't want to post something, but felt obligated to do so.

I simply told them to speak their truth. If the free book didn't align with what they wanted to read, to promote, to speak about on social media, not sharing it was okay.

The first step in building our fence is to focus on ourselves and find out what kind of house we are. To do this, we need to shine truth into the dark places inside.

To do this, I invite you to look at your life, your relationships, and list five things that don't serve you anymore.

Five things that aren't true to who you are or who you want to be.

Five truths that will help you build your fence.

Once those truths are written—we start with five, but you can add more later on—it's time to respect yourself and follow through.

As much as setting boundaries for others is hard,

respecting ourselves and following through so we don't end up with a Swiss cheese fence can be harder.

For example, one of my truths was that I needed to write poetry and not get too much into my head about what others thought about it. Remember in chapter five when I mentioned the hell I was stepping into unknowingly? When I was doing what I thought at the time was a good thing when I started writing romance? Well, this was what had ruined my pleasure in writing romance. I had been way too attached to what people thought, reading reviews and asking my team if the book was good enough.

When I followed my truth and published my second collections of poems, I built a boundary with people around me. It might have been hard for them, but their opinion, their reviews, their interpretation, didn't count that much anymore. But to really embrace that boundary I was creating, I needed to be the one stopping the validation Monster to feed on my soul. So, I stopped looking at Goodreads and reviews on Amazon. I asked some people to read my book in advance and to review it because I needed reviews, but if they didn't do so, I didn't get upset. I barely sent free books anymore, not wanting to be waiting in the expectation of someone's words nor wanting to be indebted in relationships that I felt were unbalanced.

It was a huge step for the love junkie I was, but I felt so much freer.

Then I went further and set boundaries on social media. I muted or blocked some users because I needed my peace. I didn't want to see that they supported so-and-so and not me. I didn't want to be hurt. I didn't want to feel rejected when it had nothing to do with me. When others blocked me, I accepted it. It was their boundary, and I didn't need an explanation. I didn't want drama. I didn't want anyone who didn't understand me or didn't support my transformation to be around me. I didn't want to fight to be heard and loved.

Not anymore.

In the end, I set boundaries with myself and it helped me find a certain calmness. And by saying "no more"— even if it was to myself— I chose me repeatedly.

By not saying "whatever" anymore, or saying it rarely —I still fight it from time to time—I spoke up and built my fence.

By speaking up about my truths, walking away from friends and family who couldn't align with who I was becoming, by focusing on what I wanted my journey to be and being unapologetic about it, I found my people. I learned to trust again. I saw those who were wearing a mask the way I used to, and now I could decide if I wanted to be part of their story or not. And, I wasn't making that decision because I was craving love, but because I was disentangling my authenticity from the ropes and bound I had tied myself into to get my dose of love.

By stepping outside and building fences around what is important to me—something I've done many times in recent years—I found my voice again and learned to communicate in a healthy way with my friends and children. I also found a community who supports me, friends who love me no matter what, and most important of all, I found myself.

So, here is your next step.

Exercise 9: Hold yourself accountable

Now that you wrote those five things that aren't serving you anymore, make a pact with yourself and hold yourself accountable. Here is a template you can use.

Dear (insert your name)

I will speak my truths to the best of my abilities every time I need to. I will say no to events, discussions, and people that don't resonate with me. I will back out of relationships and behaviors that don't serve me anymore. I will respect myself and my feelings so I can grow and protect myself.

I will set boundaries with myself, with others, with my kids, with my family, with my spouse, with my work, on social media...wherever I need to.

I will build a fence and not a wall.

I will protect my peace, my worth, my light and love, and respect myself daily.

This is a choice I can make and a choice I will make for me.

Sign here:

For this pact to work, you need to understand that what others think of you, how others act towards you, is only a reflection of themselves. It has nothing to do with you. Nothing at all.

I used to wonder why people treated me like this or like that, and I lost myself in the silence of a few. But I soon understood that it's because they feel unworthy themselves and because they are at war with their own minds that they treat people in a certain way.

It's okay to take time for you, to build a fence to protect yourself, to have people misunderstand you. Keep your energy for people who can hear what you have to say. Respect yourself and your own boundaries. Don't hush your voice for those who can't hear you anyway. Don't scream your worth if they stay silent.

The deaf can't hear you even if you scream... Or let me rephrase, those who are deafened by the noise of their own insecurities, by the shouts of the rowdy passengers on their own bus, can't hear you even if you scream.

I know it's a hard concept. I still sometimes catch myself wanting to reach out to someone who has given me months of the silent treatment. I did it a few times, and in the end, I just let myself down and had to pick up the pieces of my own disappointment. I then needed to realign, to remember all that I speak about in this book, to calm my Monster of unworthiness, to soothe the wound of addiction, and to forgive myself

I want to help you fight this search for approval we often fell into. To do so, I have prepared a little meditation that I recommend you record on your phone, and then let it guide you.

Close your eyes and let your emotions go through you.

Take a big breath and think of a time you yearned for approval.

Try to feel the emotions arise.

Breathe in and release your breath in a big sigh.

Breathe in again and release another sigh so your emotions can pass through you.

Take another big breath, and let go once more.

Now visualize yourself sitting under a globe of white light.

Think of the five truths you wrote down before and the fence you need to build to protect them.

Say each of your truths out loud, and every time, envision light embracing you.

Take a deep breath and let the light shower you.

Then, say:

"What people say I am

is a manifestation of their own thoughts.

It says more about them than about me.

I protect my peace,

my truths,

my worth

and my light.

And with this breath,

I let go and build my fence.

I respect and love myself, and I act like I do.

I respect and love myself, and I act like I do so.

I respect and love myself, and I act like I do."

Take a breath in and let it out. Come back to your body and open your eyes when you are ready.

Now, close the book and write down how you will honor yourself from now on. Sign and date it.

Reread the contract you wrote with yourself before this meditation. If you haven't already, sign and date it, too. Come back to it every time you need to, and remember that letting go of a boundary is letting go of yourself.

Strong isn't enough to describe her...
Hell survivor
Scar mender
Truth roarer...
Is what she is
But foremost...
She can tame love.

Gabrielle G.

Amour was my teacher
But fear was my armour
So I lost the "our"
And became love.

Gabrielle G.

Chapter 10

Stay you

Let yourself feel
Let yourself heal
Cry a thousand rivers
Recite a billion prayers
And leave behind what doesn't serve you
Kill your old self and always fight through

Gabrielle G.

This last chapter was a long time coming. It took me weeks to write it. Life caught up and I was stuck. I was stuck because I knew what I wanted to say, but I felt like an imposter for not living it fully. I had fallen into the back of the bus with all my doubts, the imposter syndrome snapping at me while my Monster was gloating.

So, I did what every writer will do when they are struggling with their mental health and deeply doubting their ability to write and share their story: I reread this whole book.

As a writer, every time you read what you wrote, you try to write it better. I usually never look at the structure of my draft before I finish writing it because if I did, I would get stuck in the first chapter. This was something I did early on in my writing career, and this is why my old computer is filled with first chapters of books that will never see the light of the day.

So, because my Monster had found a way out and was very happy to be dancing on the grave of my confidence, I rewrote most of the chapters. What my Monster didn't plan on was that my own words, the journaling exercises I created and meditations I planned in this book, would help me get out of the funk.

I know I am worthy of writing this book. Everyone is worthy of sharing their stories and helping others, and I was no exception.

I was strong enough to have gone through all of this, and vulnerable enough to put it all out there for others to help them find their way on the journey of self-love.

I was proud of my words and happy to see how everything brought me to that moment. Because, yes, I had been doubting and not pouring so much self-love in my own cup. I was going through a difficult time with my oldest and worrying too much, like most mothers do. I was tired emotionally, and sad that someone had rejected my friendship offer. But this book recentered me and reminded me that, as Wayne Dyer said, "If you change the way you look at things, the things you look at change. "

For most of my life, I felt like I wasn't chosen. I never got a proposal to get married, it was more of a de facto act. People who I considered my best friends were always telling me about their struggles with others who they considered their best friends—even if they were kind of terrible with each other. Men always chose other women over me and I always felt left behind. I was so deep into that narrative that I never saw the people who did choose me. I was too focused on those rejections to see their acceptance.

One day, as I was talking with my best friend (outside of myself) about people using silence as a punishment for something I didn't even know I needed to be punished for, and how I was fed up with not ever feeling chosen, I decided I was going to choose myself once and for all.

The next day, I simply told myself that I was chosen. It became a kind of mantra and it gave me a self-assurance that I didn't think I could find in my own words.

I let go of anyone who didn't fit the me I saw in this new narrative. They could go find another person to disrespect after all. I deserved to be chosen, and so was I.

Then, I added to my narrative that I was loved. As I said, I'm a pretty good person. I have flaws of course, but I care about people, and I do whatever I can to help anyone who needs help (though, now, I make sure that helping them doesn't violate my own boundaries).

I continued adding to my list.

I was understood.

I had always felt misunderstood since I was a little girl, so this one took me a little longer to integrate. I was told through the years that I was too artsy, too young, too tall, too blond, too everything to ever feel understood, but I knew that some people got me. I was surrounded by energies that aligned with mine. I was meeting new people who shared my spirituality, or my newfound love of myself, and sharing my journey with those people was always such a lesson and a true source of joy. In those moments, I knew I was understood, and that was now a big part of my daily life.

I was seen and heard. I wasn't invisible or mute anymore. Even if some people tried to reject my existence with their silence, ignored me, or stopped supporting me, or even worse let others believe I was the crazy one, I knew the truth, and most importantly, I knew *my* truth. I'd fought my anxiety, my demons, my wounds, my so-called insecurities, and I was strong, and loud, and colorful because I was me, and no one could take this from me.

Most of all, I was wanted. And, as a woman, this is an important statement. It is not because your current partner isn't looking at you like you are the apple of his eyes, or because your past partner went with someone else, that you aren't wanted. Your confidence, your desirability, your sexiness has nothing to do with whoever is showing interest in you—or not showing interest in you, if that is the case.

You are wanted because you are a beautiful soul that

has found a human skin, a body with sexual desires and fantasies that need to be fulfilled. If you aren't the cup of tea for one person, you will be the perfect cup for others. And, in the meantime, love yourself in the most sinful way... It's okay. You deserve to feel sexy, and wanted, and to get there, you need to want yourself. You need to look at yourself in the mirror and feel sexy. Do whatever you need to do to feel that way. I did, and I still do.

The moment that I changed my way of thinking, everything changed. I was sending such a high vibration into the world that I shone everywhere.

Jobs started to align, new friends came in, joy was in the smallest things such as the smell of Earl Grey tea with cream, and no one could make me feel small. I realized that I had never lost friends; they had lost me. They had lost a loyal, understanding, and loving soul, and no one could ever replace me in their life. I had become my own best friend, and I loved myself in a total different way than I ever had before.

I didn't wonder anymore about others. I focused on my path, my life, my journey, and whatever or whoever didn't serve my new narrative could stay on the starting line while I was chasing my dreams.

Of course, there were days that I felt like everything was crumbling. But, when I felt so desperate and so tired, I sat on a meditation pillow, took a big breath, and remembered that I was chosen, I was loved, I was understood, I was heard and seen, and I was wanted. And I repeated that to myself until I felt aligned and filled with love again.

Just writing these words for you, I feel a burst in energy and a total shift in my mindset. I am being reminded that you can shift everything, even a timeline, as easily as you snap your fingers.

I am chosen, and so are you.

So, tell me, what old story do you keep telling yourself that needs to be released? What adjectives have you have carried in your heart since childhood that your inner child needs you to heal? What is the story you need to rewrite so you can empower yourself, and grow, and shine, and become this colorful burst of happiness?

It's okay not to have it all figured out, but remember, the thoughts you put out there become your reality. I'm not asking you to be fake and to push away your emotions. I'm saying that you need to be aware of what you are thinking, of what you are putting out there, so you can change the narrative, shift your mindset, and love yourself even more. And in no time, everything will change, and you will glow from within with a light that you have ignited. And, this light can't be blown out by anything or anyone but you. So don't dull your own shine... become the candlestick that supports the light, and find the words that will help you sparkle.

You are worth loving yourself and shining bright and high. Never, ever, forget it.

Exercise 10: Final meditation for self love

For this last exercise, I want you to sit comfortably and remember our first exercise. You had two sides of yourself. The dominant one was the not so nice side of you, driven by your Monster, and the shy side was the one who was ready to give you unconditional love.

My hope is that by the end of this book, the dominant side of you is now the loving one and you can see how wonderful, powerful, incredible, and unique you are.

If that it is not the case yet, don't despair. Go back to the chapters you feel you need the most, and do the exercises and meditations again. Take your time. Be gentle with yourself. Loving yourself is also giving yourself time to adjust to loving yourself. I know it may sound like a stupid over-thinking circle, but it is one of the most important lessons here: give yourself some time, be gentle with yourself, be patient with yourself, don't judge yourself.

Back to our last exercise... Sit comfortably and call back the harsh side of you from the first exercise. Summon your Monster. Imagine it standing in front of you with their severe eyes and venom dripping off its lips. Take a minute to acknowledge what you are feeling as you look at your Monster.

Take a big breath in and let it go.

Smile at this side of you. Look at it with gentle and kind eyes, and smile bright. Imagine light coming from inside you and shining on its darkness.

Take a big breath in and let go.

With a smile on your lips, say out loud, "I forgive you."

Breathe in from your nose and let it go from your mouth. Let it all go in a deep sigh, and smile.

Now say:

"I love you.

You are extraordinary.

I love your body.

I love your laugh.

I love your tears.

I love your heart.

I love your soul.

I love your mistakes.

I love your light.

I love your darkness.

I love everything about you.

I love you.

Just the way you are.

I love you just the way you are."

Take a big breath in and, while releasing it, say:

"I love you. I love me. We are one."

See the transformation. Every time you shine light on your darkness, on your Monster, you glow even more and pour more love into your own cup.

Take one last breath in and out, and once you feel like you are at peace with yourself, journal about how you feel.

Write down the good feelings you are experiencing and stay there. Love yourself through the process, hug yourself if you need to.

Go spoil yourself as a reward of all the work you did while reading in this book.

As a final word, I want to tell you that I'm proud of you for taking this journey. I know how hard it is to love yourself. I know it's a daily battle, and I don't pretend that this book is a magical remedy, but I truly believe that by reading it, you have taken the first step on the everlasting journey of self-love.

Never hesitate to reach out through social media and come share your journey in my reader's group. It's only by supporting each other that we can truly see how wonderful and unique we are.

With love, I now invite you to close this book and go on with your life, never forgetting to choose yourself first,

to always love yourself, and to forever find and follow
your truth.

My smile was all arrows and shield
Protecting my depression
While my armour took the lead
In my self-depreciation
I was a knight of deep sarcasm
A fighter of all truth
I was afraid of my own chasm
And slowly became a sleuth
Someone else becoming
Was my way to survive
While my thoughts were brewing
And barely keeping me alive
As predicted I fell deep
And sunk in fakeness and lies
Allowing those I love to reap
The only hope in my eyes
While I crawl with bleeding knees
Trusted demons looking like friends
They choked me until I wheezed
But I fought back and made amends
And I got rid of my addictions
Found my worth in my own voice
Met people with compassion
Understanding my silences' noise
And step by step, I held my ground
Burnt from hell, I flew to faith

My words became my healing crown
And my lipstick, my shield's wraith
And now I smile with no purpose
Only because I am happy
As I tend to my thorns and rose
I love myself authentically

Gabrielle G.

Merci, etc....

This book would have never seen the light of day without the following people.

Without Jen, my actual best friend, who listened to me hours after hours in the darkest of times and reminded me I was strong enough.

Without Sanela, who encouraged me to walk my path and befriended me when others walked away.

Without Stela, who always checked on me when I didn't check on myself.

Without Sam, who was always #TeamGab.

Without Caitlin, Summer, and Bozena, who checked up on me and understood what was happening.

Without my beautiful, smart, strong, and amazing children, Ella, Arthur, and Zab, who hugged me when I needed it and spent time with me even when they didn't want to.

Without my therapist, who called me out when I was lying to myself.

Without the romance readers who stuck with me when I changed genre.

Without the friends who anchored me in the real world and the new friends who came along the way.

Without my spirits, guides, and angels who saved my

life, brought books to my attention when I needed them the most, and reminded me of who I was and how I could get there.

Without Rachel Pass, who entered my world with this book and who I hope won't leave it as I love working with her.

Thank you to each one of you. Merci de tout mon cœur.

This book is dedicated to my mother, who loved me more than the world and left us way too young.

This book is dedicated to Little Gab who craved to be loved and who finally understood that it is only by loving ourselves unconditionally that we get the dose of love we need.

This book is dedicated to each of you who read it. May you finally fall in love with yourself and slay the world.

With all my love,
Gabrielle

About the Author

Real - Raw - Authentic.

Because why write if it isn't to bleed?

Gabrielle G.'s writing is driven by pure emotion and always comes from the heart. It shines her truth, can take your breath away, and leave you wanting more, as you wipe away your tears of either sadness or laughter.

Gabrielle would do anything for a cup of tea, still celebrates her half-birthdays, and feels that everyone has an inner voice that guides our passions.

As the author of eleven romance novels and two poetry collections, Gabrielle has written this book as her testimony that everyone can learn to love themselves by working on their deepest scars and showing themselves compassion.

You can find her on Instagram (@author.gabrielle.g), Facebook and TikTok (@authorgabrielleg), and Twitter (@AuthorGabG), and subscribe to her newsletter on www.authorgabrielleg.com.

By the same author

Poetry Collections

To the man I loved too much

Melancholy & Cinnamon

Goddesses

* * *

Contemporary Love Stories

Always & Only

Never & Forever

Often & Suddenly

Heartbroken

Forsaken

Untamed

Darling

Trouble

Sweet

Mended

The Secrets We Keep

* * *

Follow Gabrielle G. on Amazon and visit her website www. authorgabrielleg.com to subscribe to her newsletter.